THE

Success
Challenge

THE
Success
Challenge

REDEFINE SUCCESS
AND BECOME EXTRAORDINARY

KRISTI STALDER

STOIC SAGE
PUBLISHING

Book, cover, and interior design by Kristi Stalder.

ISBN 979-8-9897353-0-3

Printed and bound in the United States of America.

Published by
Stoic Sage Publishing, an imprint of Stalder Books & Publishing, LLC
www.KristiStalder.com

Library of Congress Cataloging-in-Publication Data available upon request.

For all the beautiful souls on this journey:
I wish you a life just as extraordinary as you.

Contents

"People who succeed at the highest level are not lucky. They're doing something differently than everyone else."

-TONY ROBBINS

Introduction

WHERE IT ALL BEGINS

>———————————<

IF YOU'VE PICKED up this book and started reading, you've taken a deliberate step onto the path toward success. This isn't a matter of luck; it's all about the action. By choosing to seek out the knowledge and wisdom in these pages, you've already set yourself apart.

Let's be clear: this isn't a "how to be a boss babe" or "get rich quick" book. Instead, what you hold in your hands is a compass, a trusted guide meticulously crafted with the critical and necessary information that is *guaranteed* to steer you onto a successful path with actionable steps.

How can I be so certain? Because I've walked this path myself, emerging from a decade-long struggle with the weight of insurmountable debt and the grind of an unfulfilling existence. For years, I worked endlessly in the shadows of debt, pouring countless hours into making some big, powerful corporate executives' money without ever truly advancing. Life felt stagnant, devoid of freedom and happiness. I hated Sunday nights because that meant it was almost time for work on Monday. I looked forward to Fridays without appreciating the days in between, and I relished the moment that I clocked out at 5 pm.

And then, I stumbled upon the secret to success—a revelation so simple yet profoundly transformative. Looking back, I realize how this knowledge could have spared me years of hardship and misery.

The simplicity of it, this secret to success, is astonishingly powerful. Beyond the confines of my limitations, the world outside of my cage was waiting. And that little secret to success? It was the catalyst that unlocked the cage door, swinging it wide open and liberating me to spread my wings and soar toward freedom from my limitations.

The discovery was just the beginning. What followed was an intense journey of inner work and personal growth deeply rooted in the principles of entrepreneurship. These philosophies in self-mastery taught me that while we cannot control external events, we can control our reactions to them. This shift in mindset was monumental in understanding that I had the power to make the changes necessary to transform my lifestyle. Embracing these values meant acknowledging that true power lies within our own responses, attitudes, and choices.

By focusing on what I could control—my thoughts, actions, and emotions—I began to see the world differently. The obstacles that once seemed insurmountable were now viewed as opportunities for growth and learning. I took responsibility for my life and recognized that my actions and mindset were responsible for every situation I encountered. I developed core values of wisdom, courage, resilience, and restraint, which became my guiding stars, helping me navigate through life's challenges with grace.

Since discovering this secret to success, I've been living my wildest dreams. I'm free to live on my own terms, unshackled from the constraints of a 9-to-5 job. Financially, I've achieved unprecedented abundance, allowing me to invest, travel, and do things close to my heart. My relationship with my husband has been indescribably perfect, and the life we've built together continues to thrive and bring us immense joy.

It all started when I redefined success and changed my lifestyle, mindset, and habits.

This book is not just a guide to achieving external success but also to cultivating inner strength. It will teach us to find peace in the present moment, accept what we cannot change, and strive for excellence in all we do. Because living a life of virtue and purpose, regardless of the circumstances, creates genuine happiness.

Stick with me, and I promise your life will change. Success will no longer be a distant goal but a tangible reality. You'll have the tools and resources to navigate life's twists, turns, and setbacks and emerge stronger, wiser, and closer to your dreams.

At the end of each chapter, you will find an actionable To-Do list. Complete these exercises without taking any shortcuts and do them with intention in your heart. *The Success Challenge* is an opportunity to make a change in your life for the better. Stay committed, and I assure you, you'll begin to see results. Soon, you'll realize that you have the power to unlock the door to your cage and experience the freedom to live a life filled with limitless possibilities.

"It all begins when you redefine success."

—KRISTI STALDER

Chapter One

THE DEFINITION OF SUCCESS

><———————————————————<

HOW DO YOU DEFINE success? Simply put, success is the favorable or desired outcome of an action or purpose. But how do *YOU* define it? What does it mean to you personally? Would your definition include something along the lines of achieving a title or a status? Maybe it's the type of car you buy? Does it mean wealth and prosperity, respect, or fame? Accomplishing a simple or complex goal you had set? Is it a sense of achievement? A feeling?

I can't answer that for you. The definition of success lies deep in your bones, and understanding what makes it so important is the first step in any entrepreneur's adventure. It's truly subjective. My definition may be different than yours, and that's perfectly okay. We each have unique circumstances that shape our priorities differently. For some, success is putting food on the table to feed their family. For others, it's putting their children through college. And for many, success means having the freedom to spend their time and money without limits.

Finding the connection between your goals, your path to get there, and the determination to begin is where the rubber meets the road. Our maps to success will differ from anyone else's. The purpose of *The Success Challenge* is to provide strategic thinking tailored to your level of desired outcomes. This method can be applied to both big goals as well as small aspirations, providing a framework for achieving those dreams.

We can all agree that this multifaceted concept of success extends beyond wealth or public recognition. It is an ongoing endeavor, not a destination, and your definition of success may evolve over time. As you grow and your situation changes, so may your goals. They may take on a new meaning or go a completely different direction based on your new perspective.

When I had been working full-time as the Community Relations Director at an assisted living community, and someone had asked me what the definition of success was, my answer was drastically different than it is now. Before, success meant surviving. It was collecting my paycheck, paying my bills, and having some money left over for fuel and groceries. Before, success meant that I earned a title change from "manager" to "director," and my pay status bumped from hourly to salary. I thought I was so successful when I came in on a Saturday to meet with a client. I thought I was so important when I drove downtown after work for a networking meeting and got up early to attend another meeting before work began.

I was *needed*. Without my contributions, my employer would have struggled to meet their bottom line. I felt successful because they relied on me.

That was my definition of success, before.

I would still be working in that position at this very moment if it weren't for a very special person who came along at the right time and showed me his definition of success.

It seems anticlimactic, but I traced it all the way back to the very moment my life changed. It all started with an audiobook called *Rich Dad, Poor Dad* by Robert Kiyosaki. My friend had recommended it to me—rather, insisted—and while it sounded as exciting as watching paint dry, I listened to it while I drove six hours from my home in Spokane, Washington, to Salem, Oregon, on assignment to help a struggling assisted living building with its marketing efforts.

I left my house at 3 a.m. to arrive in time for their morning staff meeting at 9 a.m. I was putting in 14 hours of work that day and only getting paid for eight because I was salaried, but hey, I was important and successful because of this opportunity to travel. My ego was stoked because my experience was recognized and valued by the important corporate bosses. I mean, I was the Community Relations Director, and this was just another rung on the ladder!

During the long, lonely drive, I listened to this audiobook with raised brows and a smirk. The author talked about buying assets, investments, and financial freedom. Those words were so foreign and unrealistic at the time that I couldn't align with what they were saying. I was broke and had no intention of listening to what some rich guy was preaching. He didn't know my situation. All I could think was that this Kiyosaki guy already had lots of money, and he was telling me that I needed to spend money to make money. What a laughable concept! There was no way I could follow half of the steps he suggested, let alone put them into action. My heart wasn't in it, and I had no desire to change my current situation. I felt that I was already successful.

I finished the audiobook feeling more frustrated with the notion that I could succeed if I changed my mindset. Ha! Change my mindset? Yeah, right. It was perfect, just the way it was, thank you very much.

Even now, I cringe at the thought that I dismissed it as if I knew better. I didn't open my mind and explore options. I wasn't receptive to fresh ideas. My worldview was warped like a fish in a bowl, my capacity was capped, and my self-limiting walls were a fortress inside my mind. I desperately wish I could reach back in time to shake myself by the shoulders and tell that poor girl to simply *listen*.

A few weeks later, my friend texted me a link to a YouTube video. Curious, I opened it, and it brought me to a channel that I'd never heard of before. I set the phone on my bathroom counter and listened as I got ready for work one morning. The narrator spoke about the power of a positive mindset and habits that will change your life, blah, blah, blah...Again, it didn't interest me because I was too focused on working hard in my current director position. In my mind, I was very successful; I had a meeting with a client that day to sign paperwork and an upcoming work event to shop for, and two bosses wanted to know what my marketing outreach plans were for the week. I had better things to focus on than this ridiculous, preachy "mindset" nonsense. Nothing resonated, and again, it seemed silly to me.

As the months went by and I grew closer to this special friend, I was compelled to take another, more serious approach to what he was trying to tell me. He was so fired up and enthusiastic about these motivational videos and books that I was genuinely curious to find out why. What made them so special? Why did he connect with the messages, and I didn't?

I began listening to those motivational YouTube videos. Before work, driving to work, on my lunch break, driving home, while taking a bath...I listened to the messages with an open mind, suspending my worldview beliefs to allow the information to settle and mentally process.

And finally, I began to *hear* them.

As soon as I heard them, I started to feel *something*.

What was this indescribable feeling? This clarity, this awakening, this eagerness, this vibration in my soul; I felt as though I needed to recalibrate my life. I wanted everything that the motivational speakers were talking about. I wanted to wake up when I felt like it, not when my boss told me to. I wanted to work hard on *my* dreams and not someone else's. I wanted to spend time with my kids and not pay someone to raise them for me. I wanted financial freedom, but more importantly, I wanted *time* freedom.

Day after day, the words of Les Brown, Tony Robbins, Eric Thomas, Daymond John, Dave Ramsey, Brene Brown...their messages streamed through my speakers and straight into my soul and *SET IT ON FIRE*.

Pure, raw, unfiltered determination emanated from my very essence and took up residency in my heart. I wanted to move mountains and cross oceans. I felt as though I could do anything and everything, and my determination for this newfound definition of *success* nearly drove me crazy.

At that point in time, my definition of success transformed. No longer was it simply the desire to survive and accept recognition from corporate bosses. It morphed into an insatiable hunger to thrive and transcend limitations, break barriers, and obliterate the self-imposed limits on my capacity.

In the wake of this realization, I aligned myself with new goals to make changes in my life to find financial freedom, time freedom, and happiness. I discovered that my next step was to take action by adjusting my focus, changing my daily habits to be more productive, my lifestyle to prioritize my goals, and how I responded to situations to protect my mental well-being. I spent more time in my own mind confronting negativity and weeding out non-productive thoughts, looking for silver linings in every circumstance, and relentlessly brainstorming solutions to issues I had been dealing with rather than complaining about them.

Success is more than a definition; it's a calling, an emotional trigger for you to push through any obstacle. The call to success will reverberate through every fiber of your being, and when you hear it, the sound will consume you. Passion will awaken. Determination will begin clearing the path for action, brushing aside anything that stands in your way. Your goals will become a beacon, pulling you and guiding your heart like a moth to a flame.

Listen for it. *Hear* it. And take that first step toward it.

I challenge you to think about what success means to you. What breathes oxygen over that little ember of passion? What whispers in your ear and keeps you up at night? What areas in your life do you wish to change for the better? If you could wave a magic wand and manifest your heart's deepest desire, what would it be? What needs to happen to get there?

No matter your age, situation, or financial status, you can distinguish what success means and set the course for your goals. Are you ready for the Success Challenge? Because we're starting today.

Right now, at this very moment.

THE SUCCESS CHALLENGE #1

1. *Grab a notebook, write today's date up top, and write down your unique definition of "success." Be genuine with yourself—there are no wrong answers. Reflect on what success truly means to you and articulate it on paper. Your definition may change by the end of this book, and that's perfectly okay.*

2. *List your goals in order of importance based on your definition of success. Ensure these goals are meaningful and grounded in realism, preparing for achievable milestones within the next five years.*

3. *Next to each goal, assign a desired deadline. This simple act transforms your aspirations from abstract dreams to tangible targets and sets the stage for deliberate action.*

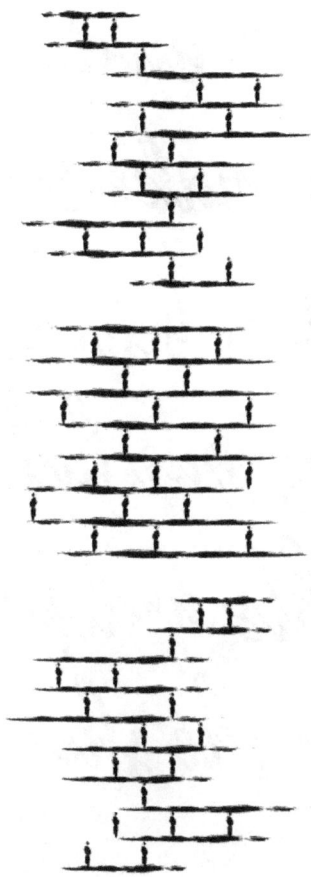

"With awareness,
we can make conscious
choices instead of
letting our habitual
thoughts and patterns
run the show."

—TAMARA LEVITT

Chapter Two

MINDSET, MINDSET, MINDSET

>———————<

THE POWER OF POSITIVE thinking is out of this world. In fact, it should be classified as a superpower because of the real changes caused by the mental processes within our brains. How incredible is that? Our brain is busy firing away electrical impulses from neuron to neuron, resulting in words, actions, and feelings. On a macro-scale, those tiny electrical impulses within our brains can literally change the world!

A single thought can trigger powerful emotions and sway the direction of those feelings by a default reaction. To put it simply, we are conditioned to think in a certain way, and we process information the way we are taught. We become a product of our environment, so our thought process comes from those with whom we spend the most time. Not only that, but our thoughts are influenced by everything around us: social media, the news, politics, school, work, and current world problems...all these things are processed in our minds, and we make subconscious choices about how we deal with them.

The key to making the right choice is in the pause. *Respond,* not react. When triggered by something and emotions flare, the best practice is to pause and take a breath. Collect our emotions, mentally put them on a leash, and tell them to settle so that you can process what is happening. *You* control your emotions, not the other way around. This is one of the most difficult actions in life, but as a fundamental concept around which you will build your thinking, you can apply this to anything you do. Whether dealing with stress, grief, tough choices, sadness, or even experiencing happiness, you must respond, not react. Controlling the impulse is the benefit. Maintaining a distinct line between logic and emotion when making decisions will prevent impulsive actions and ensure more thoughtful, effective outcomes.

The ability to pause before responding requires dedicated practice and conscious effort. With time, you will develop this habit, and it will become second nature. When situations arise that are beyond your control, this practice will give you a tremendous advantage to search for solutions and alternatives without losing yourself to your emotional reactions.

One of my favorite quotes by Marcus Aurelius is: "You have the power over your mind, not external events. Realize this, and you will have strength." A powerful concept that rings true for all of us. We cannot control what happens to us, but we can control how we react to it. The power of our mindset is something no one can ever control unless we allow it. We can make choices, and we can choose to remain in control.

So, how exactly do you develop this habit?

Practicing positive thinking involves cultivating self-awareness and mindfulness. Begin by recognizing your thoughts and emotions without judgment. When faced with challenges, pause and consider how you can respond in a way that aligns with your values and goals. Embrace the idea that you have the agency to choose your response. Is this something that really deserves your mental and emotional energy? Can you fix this situation, or is it beyond your control? What do you have to gain by emotionally reacting to it? Is this feeling of anger worth derailing your focus on what's truly important? For example, if you get stuck in traffic, you have a choice: you can either be mad about the delay, or you can let that negative thought slip away and...just *be*. Turn up the radio and go with the flow. Since you can't control the traffic, why bother reacting to it? You'll reach your destination in one of two ways: angry or calm. The choice is yours. Why not choose to stay neutral and reap the benefits?

Anger, compassion, understanding—they are all choices within your control. Developing the self-awareness to process your thoughts requires practice in discerning and managing your emotions, but it's liberating to have the capacity to quiet the negative voices within us. Like a muscle, this habit must be exercised and honed to become instinctive. Then, you can choose to see an event as it truly is: *an objective situation*. Most importantly, what you think, you become, and how you feel is determined by the opinion you choose to give the situation.

This goes together with the Law of Attraction, which uses the power of our mind to translate our thoughts and materialize them into reality—also known as *manifestation*. This concept confused me at first, and I struggled to accept the notion that whatever we think, we create. How is it possible, and if it's true, why aren't there happier people in the world creating positive outcomes?

The answer lies in the complexity of human psychology and the interplay of various factors that influence our thoughts and behaviors. While the Law of Attraction emphasizes the importance of positive thinking, it's not a magical formula that guarantees instant happiness or success. Our thoughts alone do not determine our reality; they are just one aspect of a broader concept that includes actions, external circumstances, and the influence of others. Our subconscious beliefs and conditioning dictate our thought patterns, which may not always support our conscious desires. Unresolved traumas, limiting beliefs, and societal conditioning can create internal barriers that obstruct our ability to manifest our intentions fully.

A great example of the Law of Attraction can be illustrated with a quick exercise: look around your room, find 10 red items, and say the name of each item out loud. Now, without looking up from your book, try to name 10 green items in your room. It's difficult to recall, right? By focusing on one color, our minds automatically hone in on it. Another example is thinking of a particular car model and color. Once you start driving around, you'll notice just how many of those cars in that color are on the road. This concept of the Law of Attraction applies to our goals as well. When we focus on a specific aspect of our goal, we begin to see it everywhere, thus reinforcing our attention and energy toward achieving it.

The Law of Attraction requires more than just positive thinking; it necessitates consistent action, self-awareness, and a willingness to confront and transform negative thought patterns. Many people may struggle to implement these practices consistently or may be unaware of their subconscious influences.

Take, for instance, my crippling fear of public speaking. Despite this obstacle, my heart is set on hosting workshops and events to help support fellow writers and entrepreneurs. I've become aware that my limiting beliefs are fueling this fear, and the only way I can grow through this is to face it head-on. I must demonstrate to myself that I can do it without succumbing to these undermining thoughts.

That's the point that most of us fail. We are stuck standing outside the door, knowing we must feel discomfort to proceed. Most of us balk at that discomfort. It's a default *reaction*. We subconsciously value our pain threshold over the opportunity to push past it. We allow our negative thoughts to control the outcome as if it has already happened. However, the only way to move forward on the path of success is to intentionally place ourselves in an uncomfortable state of being. Then, our mental strength grows and soon becomes a natural *response* to discomfort. Some call it self-discipline, which is, in my opinion, the highest form of self-love. It's ignoring something that you want right now for something better later. We can train ourselves to ignore intrusive thoughts and impulses in favor of delayed gratification. It reveals the commitment you have to yourself and your goals. After all, the *future* you is depending on the *current* you to keep the promises you made to yourself yesterday.

Several years ago, I manifested this book you are reading. It started with a thought, accompanied by a passion for sharing these powerful messages, and with time, determination, and self-discipline, I could see and create the end result: this book in your hands. It's not magic. It requires action and follow-through to complete the tasks and accomplish the goal.

The easy part is talking about it. It's challenging because it requires awareness, but it's all a part of holding tight to your aspiration for success. If you want it bad enough, like air when drowning, you'll do whatever it takes to achieve success.

Start today, *this moment*. Self-awareness and mindfulness. Take a deep breath and commit to making a conscious choice to become aware of your thought patterns. Prevent your negative habitual thoughts from running the show. We can't control the external events, but instead, let's look for the positive—the "plus" side—of every moment during the day. Need to mow the lawn in the sweltering heat? No worries! Not only will it look so beautiful when you're finished, you'll get some exercise, and you can enjoy a nice, cold drink when you're done. Does your boss want you to come in on your day off? It'll be okay! Think about that extra money in your paycheck. My favorite shift in thinking happens when a slow driver takes a long time to turn. I smile and pretend that a sweet, old grandma is sitting in the front seat, wearing her best dress while balancing a giant birthday cake on her lap. Sounds silly, but the thought alone prompts me to be kind and understanding because that feels much better than being angry or impatient.

Train your mind to pause for a moment, process and look for the positive, and then allow yourself to react. Hold back the negative thoughts and yank them out before they have time to trigger an emotion. It takes practice, but you'll begin to see that it gets easier in time and know it's working when you start to *feel* better.

There will be challenging times when you experience anger or resentment, or maybe you're hurt by something someone said. You know...*normal human emotions.* There's no such thing as a life without feeling negative emotions at one point or another. Remember, this is normal. You are normal. The important part is how you *react* to these negative emotions. It is during these moments that positive thinking shifts the outcomes. It will be the last thing you'll want to do, but I promise, this is where you'll experience character growth.

Don't try to change the way someone else thinks or feels. Rather, try to understand them. Oftentimes, we project our insecurities and faults upon others. Jealousy, doubt, guilt, and unhappiness are common behaviors projected by someone who has failed to change their way of thinking and their way of doing. Successful people who have outgrown friends—and even family—will recognize the lack of support or critical words used to drag them down. This comes from a place deep within the cynical people who wish for successful people's results. As hard as it may be, rise above it. Turn away from the doubt with gratitude for your personal growth, appreciate that you are building the life you want, and continue cultivating success. Look for the goodness in their hearts and hold onto that.

Keeping a positive mindset crosses over to how we interact with the world around us. When we meet someone for the first time, we generate a first-impression response. In a split second, we automatically assess that person's appearance and apply the current social-cultural standards to see if they fit the stereotypes. Each of us will have pre-determined preferences for which standards we agree or disagree with, and if this person doesn't meet our preferences based on their appearance, we make the subconscious choice to dislike and distrust this person. It's a thought pattern that we are defaulted to use, and it takes a mature awareness to change what we do with the way we respond. Instead of assuming the worst or applying a negative thought, pause a moment and collect all the attributes of this person's character from their behavior, ideas, and personality before applying assumptions. Our world is diverse and full of powerful, creative, and forward-thinking minds. Don't get caught in the undertow of judgmental thinking; it will drag you down to a level that will stunt your character growth. Be kind to everyone! Especially those with different opinions, political stances, religions, etc.

Your mindset navigates success. You are the ship's captain, and it's up to you to explore and discover ways to keep your vessel afloat when the seas are rough. You have the power and control to do anything and everything in this world.

Literally, *anything*.

No matter the physical, financial, or mental limitations, there are ways to elevate higher than those things hindering your progress. It's up to you to want it bad enough that you'll do anything to make it happen. You control the outcome. You control the journey. It all starts in your mind. A growth mindset is essential to continue to rise and keep reaching for your goals. Feed it, nurture it with rituals of positive thought patterns, and watch your spirit soar.

A positive, focused mindset is so important that highly successful people begin their mornings with self-empowerment rituals to mentally prepare themselves for the day. By establishing a routine and sticking to it, you allow yourself to begin the day with a direct focus and energy to maintain alignment with your goals. Above all, it's training for a disciplined mind to get long-lasting results.

When you wake up in the morning, begin with a grateful heart. It's scientifically tested and proven that gratitude rewires our brains for happiness and good health, and it's one of the habits that will elevate your success rate. Reconstruct your thought patterns to clear the unconstructive behaviors and emotions. You cannot feel angry and grateful at the same time!

Try this exercise and think about three things that you're thankful for and write your thoughts in a journal. I downloaded an app on my phone that sends me daily reminders and gratefulness prompts, and if I can't get to my journal, I write my thoughts within the app. Spend a few minutes thinking about three things you're thankful for—past, present, and future—and let that feeling of gratefulness purge any feelings of resentment or negativity. Get deep inside your mind and attach the emotion to that thought of gratitude. Feel it and soak it up.

Next, take a few minutes and visualize three goals you want to achieve today or in the future. Close your eyes, imagine that you've achieved those three goals, and allow yourself to celebrate that feeling of completion and victory. Visualize success and how your life will be when you accomplish those goals and manifest it within your mind. Doing this allows you to rewire your brain for success and practice the Law of Attraction. You will attract whatever it is you're focusing on.

This practice of starting your day with a routine isn't about the routine itself. Rather, it's about gaining and growing a successful mentality. Forcing yourself to wake up early is hard because we would rather be comfortable sleeping in our beds. Obviously. But discipline and willpower are only sharpened by remaining consistent and getting up early, even when you don't want to.

I challenge you to create your own daily routine to develop your growth mindset. Start when you wake up tomorrow morning and commit to maintaining it consistently. The first few days will be easy, but it will get harder. Stay strong!

Remember, it's just as hard *not* to do it.

Pick your hard.

THE SUCCESS CHALLENGE #2

1. *In your notebook, identify what self-imposed limitations you've encountered—be completely honest with yourself. What excuses do you tell yourself that are preventing you from succeeding in life? What habits are you struggling to drop? Why can't you accomplish your goals? What barriers are in your way? Write them down.*

2. *Identify the first limitation. Then, brainstorm three ways that you could work around this issue. Reflect on the setback or obstacle and reframe it as an opportunity for growth. Ask yourself how you can prioritize and create the time for it. How can you find the energy? How can you find the resources? Resist the temptation to create new excuses; instead, commit this space solely to generating solutions. Guard your mental landscape against negative thought patterns and affirm that where there's a goal, there's unquestionably a path to achievement.*

"If you want to catch a cold, hang out with sick people. If you want to lose, associate with losers. But if you want to become successful, go out of your way to associate with successful people."

—THOMAS STANLEY

Chapter Three

YOUR INNER CIRCLE

>———————————<

YOU BECOME WHO you associate with. The people that you spend the most time with become your influencers, and whether you realize it or not, you will develop habits that mirror your friends.

Your social circle shapes your path to success in a way that either pushes you forward or holds you back, depending on the type of influence your friends have on you.

Imagine you have a friend who is an entrepreneur at heart. They're always optimistic and talking about new opportunities and ways to overcome challenges. Their positive attitude is contagious, influencing you to think along the same thought pattern to look for specific positive outcomes. You will likely never catch them complaining, rather, they would be more inclined to discuss problems and solutions.

Now, let's say you have a friend who is negative and pessimistic and complains about every inconvenience in their life. They bring you down and cast doubt on your own capabilities or potential, effectively wiping out your motivation and draining your emotional energy. It's important to note that this doesn't make them bad people; they may simply be seeking empathy for their situation rather than a solution.

I understand—we all need to vent sometimes. We need to be heard and understood. But there is a fine line between occasional venting and chronic negativity. When a friend habitually focuses on the negative aspects of life, it can create a toxic environment that hinders your own growth. Their constant complaints and pessimism can subtly influence your mindset, leading you to adopt a similarly bleak outlook on life.

It's crucial to recognize the impact that your relationships can have on your mental and emotional well-being. While it's important to be compassionate and supportive, it's equally important to protect your own energy and maintain a positive mindset. Surrounding yourself with people who inspire and uplift you will make a significant difference in your journey toward success.

Spending time with someone who is driven,

optimistic, and solution-oriented, their energy is infectious. They encourage you to see *opportunities* rather than obstacles and to focus on your strengths rather than weaknesses. Their influence will boost your confidence, enhance your motivation, and help you develop a growth mindset. Who wouldn't want at least 10 friends like that?

On the other hand, spending too much time with someone who is perpetually negative has the opposite effect. You will find yourself focused on problems rather than solutions, feeling more stressed and less capable. Over time, this can erode your confidence, and your progress will stall.

It's not about abandoning friends who are going through tough times. Rather, it's about setting boundaries and ensuring that you also surround yourself with people who contribute positively to your life. Encourage your negative friends to look for constructive ways to address their issues or respond to gossip with compliments about the person instead. Meanwhile, make a conscious effort to seek out and engage with individuals who inspire and motivate you.

By doing so, you'll create a balanced support system that maintains your growth while still being there for those who need you. Choose to be around those who lift you up, and you'll find it easier to rise to your full potential.

I learned this lesson the hard way, and by the time I made the choice to cut a toxic person out of my life, I grieved as if it were a death, as it truly was the death of a relationship.

When I was in high school, I didn't have a lot of friends. I was always busy, and my schedule didn't allow much free time. I attended a few classes at my high school in the morning and finished the day at my community college. Then, it was off to the horse barn for chores and riding. When I was done there, I'd race back home and get started on my homework. No time for socializing, no time for friends. Just work, work, work.

Sure, I had friends at school. But I had an incredible best friend who lived right across the street from me. She loved books just like me, and we had everything in common.

We were inseparable.

For years, we spent our weekends hanging out, talking about boys, books, and any issues we were dealing with. She was my support system, and I was hers.

As teenage girls do, we dressed the same, styled

each other's hair, went to the movies, hung out at the mall (back when it was cool), and paraded around in our happy little world. Looking back, I loved the feeling of sharing a childhood with someone who had similar values. She understood me in a way that no one else had. We shared the bond of sisters, and I loved her as such.

Life was great!

Until it wasn't.

Things started to shift when we got a little older, and I started my senior year of high school while she was a junior. I had gotten into a semi-serious relationship at that point, and we began to spend our free time without each other. My focus was on my studies and my love life, and while I didn't love my friend any less, she felt like I was pushing her away.

Before long, we hardly saw each other at all. Between work and school, relationships, and my horse, there was no time left to maintain what we had before.

We remained friends for years after graduation, but there was always an unspoken tension between us, with an undertone of jealousy. No matter how hard I tried to boost her up and share the excitement of all the good life changes that were taking place, she was anything but supportive.

Her life was untethered from goals and dreams, while mine was tied down to a job and aspirations. Our paths diverged, but I clung to that relationship like a ship dragging an anchor.

Then, she disappeared.

Through word of mouth, I gathered that she moved away to be with her estranged mother, and she didn't even say goodbye. Her phone didn't work, and I had no way of contacting her.

My heart was shattered, and I missed her so much. All I could do was wait until she reached out to me.

Some of our mutual friends shared bits and pieces about who my best friend truly was while I wasn't around, and that cut deeper than anything. After hearing the terrible things she said about me, it was clear that she projected her jealousy, faults, and insecurities on me, and I refused to believe any of it.

So, I held on.

Years went by, and she reappeared on social media. After all this time, we finally met up, and I hugged her as if I would never let go. We spent time catching up on life, and I discovered that she had moved out of the country. When she left for home, I promised that I would find a way to visit her.

Shortly afterward, I got my passport. I was going to fulfill my promise and see my best friend who I loved dearly.

Then, the relationship took a final turn. She had seen a picture on my social media of my newest relationship, and she blew up. In the harshest words, she questioned why she—my best friend—didn't know who this man was and why I hadn't told her of my recent life changes. It was so out of character that I assumed she was joking, and I typed a reply that she didn't have a phone for me to call and tell her the news. When I got no response after that, it dawned on me that it was finally time to let her go.

That decision was the most difficult one I've made in my life. Bigger than any life change to date.

I *had* to let her go.

She was toxic to me. She planted doubts and brought out my insecurities, making me question my worth and my path. Our reunion had stirred up old wounds, reminding me of the emotional turmoil I endured over the years. As much as I wanted to hold on to the memory of our friendship, I realized that clinging to it was holding me back. Rather than focusing my energy on my goals, I felt drained and edgy from trying to maintain a relationship that was no longer healthy.

In letting her go, I chose to prioritize my well-being and growth. It wasn't easy. The bond we shared had been significant, and the loss felt like a death. Yet, I knew that to move forward, I needed to surround myself with positivity and support, not with someone who dragged me down. I miss her still, even to this day.

The decision to sever ties with her marked a turning point in my life. I started focusing on relationships that nurtured and uplifted me. I sought out friends who inspired and encouraged me, who celebrated my successes, and who supported me through challenges. In time, I found peace in my new circle. Letting go of that toxic relationship was an act of self-preservation, and it allowed me to reclaim my confidence and refocus on what really mattered. It taught me the importance of choosing the right people to share my journey with—those who truly have my best interests at heart.

This experience was a reminder that while letting go can be painful, it is sometimes necessary for our own growth and happiness. Real friends will celebrate your milestones, and fake friends avoid acknowledging them. Real friends compliment you when you're not there, while fake friends criticize you when you're not around.

When you find yourself in deep water with someone who can't swim, thrashing around, refusing a life jacket, and each time you try to help, they drag you down into the abyss; you must accept that they cannot be saved. You must break free of their grip to save yourself. Letting go of toxic relationships is respecting our personal values and staying true to our principles.

Take a deep breath and distance yourself from those you've outgrown and who have been most unsupportive. Then, celebrate those who are your true friends and hold them close to your heart.

THE SUCCESS CHALLENGE #3

1. *Take a moment to reflect on the individuals who make up your inner circle—your friends, family, and mentors. How have these relationships evolved? Evaluate your inner circle for toxic relationships. Recognize patterns of negativity, unsupportive behavior, or criticism. Maintain awareness of how this person interacts with you and note how they make you feel. Are they draining your energy or energizing you? Do they sow doubt or lift you up? Reflect on when to pivot—when to outgrow, when to distance from toxicity, and when to intentionally surround yourself with positive, uplifting souls.*

2. *Celebrate positive influences and focus on the positive people within your inner circle. Express gratitude to those who genuinely support your dreams, offer constructive feedback, and inspire you. Acknowledge the significance of being surrounded by individuals who contribute positively to your life. If critical voices are in your inner circle, consider your options for prioritizing your well-being.*

"99% of the failures come from people who have the habit of making excuses."

—GEORGE W. CARVER

Chapter Four

FIND A MENTOR, FOLLOW A MENTOR

PICTURE YOURSELF TRUDGING through a dense forest in the dark. You only have a flashlight to see a few feet before you as you step over unknown terrain with only the moon as your guide. It's frightening, to say the least, not knowing if you'll step on a snake coiled in the grass or stumble over a fallen log.

Now, imagine a seasoned explorer joining you on this walk. They carry a flashlight and a detailed map of the forest, having walked this path countless times before. They know where the hidden pitfalls lie and where the ground is solid. They understand the sounds of the forest and can decipher whether they hear danger or simply the ambiance of the night.

A mentor is that seasoned explorer. They clear your path with their experience, helping you traverse the complexities with their insight and guidance.

We *need* mentors.

Not only for professional advice but also for learning important life lessons, emotional support, and personal growth. They empower you to believe in yourself, guide you toward the desired result, and demonstrate the skills required for success.

Speaking from personal experience, a mentor can change the entire trajectory of your life. They can stop you from spinning uncontrollably on your axis, tilt you on the right course, and give you a little push.

I wish I had figured this out long before I got caught up in my former broke-minded lifestyle. My perspective on the world was distorted, and I had been living my life for all the wrong reasons. As an independent teenager, I had moved out of my parent's house a month before graduating high school, convinced that I was ready to take on the world. For several years, I lived an unchanging routine of working the late-night shift at McDonald's, watching TV until the sun came up, and then sleeping until I had to get ready for work the next evening. The worst part was living paycheck to paycheck without a single thought for my future.

It was an absolute waste of my prime.

Looking back, I realize how different my life could

have been with a mentor's guidance. A mentor could have helped me see beyond my immediate circumstances, inspired me to pursue my true potential, and set me on a path toward success. I could have developed a skill set, learned a trade, started a business, or simply saved money. That time spent watching worthless television dramas and spending money on unnecessary luxuries makes me cringe. I drifted aimlessly, completely unaware of the opportunities I was missing and the time I was wasting.

Time that I'll never get back.

Fast-forward ten years, and I found myself working in an assisted living facility, earning a comfortable living, and accomplished in my role as a community relations director. It was during this time that I found my mentor, and life immediately shifted course.

This person came into my life seemingly out of nowhere, and at first, I was drawn to his values and confidence. When he spoke, there was strength and power in his words and not a word of negativity or cynicism. It was refreshing to hear someone speak and not focus on the terrible things that happened that day, or how tired he was, or how he couldn't wait for the weekend to come. Instead, our conversations were exciting, about the very best things that happened that day, what we were most grateful for, and our plans for working toward a specific goal. It wasn't just exciting...it was electrifying. I would listen to him speak about how he had solved a challenge—they were never called "issues" or "problems"—and what his next steps were.

Without realizing it, this friend had become my mentor. He had effectively inspired me to change my thought patterns and look for positivity in situations. His influence made me want to be more like him—ambitious, determined, and genuinely happy. He empowered me to articulate my future goals and, through constructive conversations, walked me through the steps I could take to get there.

No one had ever motivated me to become a better person quite like this. Because of this mentor, my definition of success had changed. My entire life ground to a halt, and rather than spinning that meaningless lifestyle back into the old rotation, I used his teachings to turn it in a completely different direction.

Mentorship has been a cornerstone in the business world for many recognizable names. One of my favorite motivational speakers, Jim Rohn, has philosophies on personal development, financial independence, and self-discipline that have profoundly impacted me. Rohn taught me that success leaves clues, meaning that by studying the habits of successful people, one can replicate their success. I took this advice to heart, modeling my strategies on the principles I learned from my mentor.

Through my mentor's experiences, I learned which mistakes to avoid along the way. I clung to his every word, read every book he recommended, and listened to every podcast or YouTube video he suggested. I gained so much mental clarity, and because I respected this person so much, I subconsciously began to mirror and practice his habits. What a phenomenal change it was! During the day, my colleagues would say things like, "I've never seen you look so happy!" and "It's so good to see you smiling!" My mentor showed me that I already had the discipline and determination within, and he inspired me to shift my thinking to see the world through clear and focused lenses. He led me to find my voice and helped me discover that I can accomplish absolutely anything. I began to pay off my debt and started writing my first book, and my weekend photography business had a waiting list.

Looking back, I don't believe I would have gotten

out of my slump if it weren't for an outside influence. I was too comfortable, too naïve, and untrained in the world of successful living. My first step toward change was being receptive and open to hearing from a different perspective. I suspended my judgment and personal opinions and took the time to listen.

One of the best pieces of advice I've gotten was, "Don't listen to people whose life you don't want to live." In other words, don't take guidance from people who are broke, miserable, and unsuccessful because you will be mirroring their habits and adopting their mindset that has led to their results. Instead, tune into those who have what *you* want. Focus on individuals who have put in the work to reach their goals and are willing to help you achieve yours, as well.

I worked with a book coaching client who shared that her family doubted her desire to become a children's book author. They told her she was wasting her time and should focus on her work and more practical matters. It saddened me to hear this because our loved ones should support our dreams. Yet, sometimes, they unwittingly carry voices of discouragement.

Don't listen to those voices.

Find a mentor who has walked the path you're

on. Surround yourself with the individuals whose lives reflect the success and fulfillment you envision for yourself. Let their voice fill your mind with encouragement, determination, and discipline. Hear their voice through a filter of nothing but guidance and wisdom toward your goals. After all, behind every successful person is a mentor who believed in them before they believed in themselves.

THE SUCCESS CHALLENGE #4

1. *Search YouTube for "Motivational Speakers" and "Motivation Madness." Pick two or three videos and listen without any distractions. Then, in your notebook, write down the names of the speakers you found to be most inspiring. What message resonated with you the most? Who said it? How does it make you feel listening to them?*

2. *Research these motivational speakers. Learn their stories and how they rose to success. Why do they share their messages with us? What changed their lives? How did they transform themselves? Dive deep and look for similarities within yourself. What drives you? What echoes in your life as in theirs?*

3. *Read, read, read. There are countless self-development books that can help you grow. Develop a habit of reading at least one chapter a day. Audiobooks are an excellent alternative for multitaskers.*

"A goal without a plan is just a wish."

—ANTOINE DE SANT-EXUPERY

Chapter Five

DEVELOP YOUR ACTIONABLE PLAN

IN THE BIG picture of achieving success, the pivotal moment arrives when your aspirations transition from hopes, dreams, and wishes into well-defined goals. We've all had those moments when we contemplate a career change, envision something new, or offer a service that could bring in substantial income. Maybe you've watched a fancy car drive down the road and imagined yourself behind the wheel, choosing which color you'd want. They're all just hopes and dreams—until you take the reins and develop the plan to make them a reality. This is where your power lies in shaping your own journey toward success.

Some of our aspirations are so grand that it feels like they're just a dream. But the surprising truth is that you already have the essential tools to start. The boat—

no, the mega-yacht—for this daunting expedition is your *plan*, a map that guides you through the unpredictable currents of challenges. And just as a ship needs a clear course, your goals require a structured plan to steer you toward success. Without this, you'll spend your time floating around in the endless ocean of opportunities. (Although I wouldn't mind floating around on a yacht...)

You wouldn't get into that fancy car and start driving before determining where you're going, so let that concept apply to your life. Establish a plan for each goal and decide which steps are necessary to get to where you want to be.

How, exactly, do we do this, especially if we're exploring uncharted water and have no experience knowing which way to go?

The idea is to start small and generalize. You'll fill in the blanks and pivot as you go, but scratch out a general plan onto paper. This initial step involves breaking down the parameters into manageable components. Consider this phase as laying the foundation for your dreams. Define the scope of your ambition by identifying what you aim to achieve, the scale of your goals, and the limits you are willing to reach. Then, begin delineating the specific tasks and milestones into manageable actions and setting measurable targets along the way. By doing so, you deconstruct the overarching goal into a series of achievable steps.

Antoine De Saint-Exupéry's quote is another one of my all-time favorites: "A goal without a plan is just a wish." This emphasizes the importance of assigning *deadlines* to each aspect of your plan. Deadlines act as the driving force because you're placing an expectation onto yourself that you strive to meet. Establishing reasonable timeframes for each task injects a sense of urgency and commitment, pushing you to take consistent action.

This idea is how I made this book you're reading a reality. I started with a goal; to write a book. Then, I created a chapter outline summarizing the messages I wanted to convey. I calculated a reasonable timeframe that could be accomplished by breaking my writing sessions into small chunks of time. Finally, I just *began*.

This approach transformed the monumental task of writing a book into a series of achievable daily goals, making the entire process less overwhelming. I knew what result I wanted. After several months of writing, I finished my rough draft and designed the cover. I laid out a marketing strategy and prepared promotional materials. With everything in place, I continued according to my well-thought-out plan, confident in the path I had charted to bring this book into the world.

Perhaps the most relatable part of anyone's journey is when we don't feel motivated. Feelings get in the way, priorities get in the way, and some days, we don't have the focus to churn out anything of value. This happened a lot during the months of writing.

Life got in the way of my goal.

At the end of the day, I was not motivated to sit down and write. The day's challenges had drained my mental energy, my kids had utterly exhausted me, and I wanted nothing more than to indulge in activities that didn't require thinking.

But that's where my growth happened.

I made myself sit down and write, even when I didn't feel like it. I pushed through the urge to "just do it tomorrow," and I had a breakthrough each time. Most nights, I would drag myself to bed at 2 am after writing for hours.

My self-imposed deadline was approaching, and I needed that last little push to finish it in time. Just a bit more pressure to hyperfocus my energy on getting it done. So, I promoted the upcoming launch. On the first day that I posted about it on my social media, the pre-orders flowed in! Now, my deadline had a real financial impact, and it drove me to work hard on getting it done to fulfill my promises to my readers and myself. You're reading this because I followed an actionable plan. I developed and executed this plan, and the results are tangible.

It's important to recognize that a plan is not a rigid constraint but a guide. Unforeseen challenges and changing circumstances are inherent in any plan. Be open to adjustments as needed, and remember to be flexible. In fact, adjustments to your plan are to be *expected*. It's rather unheard of to work toward something and not have to change things around to accommodate forces beyond our control. The beauty of a well-constructed plan lies in its adaptability. Like adjusting the sails in response to the wind, you can tweak your plan to navigate unexpected twists and turns to keep that forward progress.

Developing an actionable plan is not a theoretical notion but a tried-and-true practical approach meant to be personalized. A sense of accomplishment results as the daily goal is reached, like checking off a task on your to-do list. This systematic progress reinforces a positive feedback loop, motivating you to tackle the next phase. The process continues as you refine and adjust your plan based on real-time feedback and insights gained along the way. It, too, evolves alongside your growth and adapts to the changing landscape.

If you get stuck planning things out, try working backward, beginning with the end result. Strategize how long each process will take and what resources are needed. It's okay not to know everything that is needed to get there. You'll discover these things as you go. Just the idea of a beginning, middle, and end to accomplish that goal is needed, along with deadlines to strive for. The rest of the plan will emerge once put into action. If the plan doesn't work, change the plan, not the goal. Of course, determination, discipline, and ambition are the fuel for turning your plan into a reality. They provide the *momentum* needed to create your outcomes.

The simple truth is if you fail to plan, you plan to fail. So, write it all down on paper.

Stop wishing and start planning!

THE SUCCESS CHALLENGE #5

1. In your notebook, develop your actionable plan and articulate the actionable steps you will take toward your goal(s). Break down each goal into manageable tasks and summarize the key steps and priorities. This visual represents your intentional and focused approach, providing clarity on the path ahead.

2. Next to each goal, assign a desired deadline. Understand that these timeframes should be realistic and adaptable.

3. List your goals in order of importance based on your evolving definition of success. Recognize that priorities may shift over time, and you must revisit and adjust your list accordingly. By prioritizing, you create a focused approach, directing your energy toward the most significant goals of your success challenge. Remember, it is a continuous and evolving process. Revisit your reflections and adjustments regularly.

"*You must gain control over your money, or the lack of it will forever control you.*"

—DAVE RAMSEY

Chapter Six

FINANCIAL FREEDOM

>———————————<

A DECADE BEFORE I redefined success and began writing this book, I was drowning in over $200k of debt. Between a mortgage, car loans, and credit card balances, I could barely scrape together enough to put food on the table. My income was just enough to cover the minimum payments, leaving a measly hundred dollars to stretch over two weeks for fuel and groceries. I would practically foam at the mouth while waiting for my annual tax return and celebrate when I got a refund. Those refunds, an average of $3k, would be dumped onto a credit card balance, alleviating a payment of $100.00. In my mind, I was $100.00 richer every month! I planned to snowball that into another payment and chip away at the debt iceberg.

Little did I know, I was steering the ship right toward it.

During the year, I would give in to instant gratification and run out to buy whatever the bright, shiny thing was. That always resulted in another credit card balance, returning me to where I was before.

Repeat this pattern for TEN YEARS.

To make the situation worse, I had a daycare obligation for my two young kids. The average daycare cost for one month for both children was $1k. That meant my first paycheck—80 hours of work—went straight to the daycare, just so I could go to work and make another paycheck that went straight to my bills and debt. It was a pitiful way of living, but I could see no end in sight. I thought it was normal because everyone else was in debt, just like me, and they saw nothing wrong with buying things on a credit card. I mean, that was normal, right?

Absolutely not.

Debt should never be considered normal or normalized. I firmly believe that financial management should be a fundamental part of education, as it's a skill we'll all need to navigate throughout our entire lives. After all, what could be more crucial than managing the inescapable fact that money impacts every aspect of our lives?

We've been conditioned to adopt a consumer mindset. Companies make it seem effortless to buy their products by tempting us with lines of credit. "Just take it home and pay for it in small amounts over the years," they say. "You won't even notice!" Or my least favorite, the annoying sales pressure at the register when the cashier asks you three times to open an in-store credit card. "You can pay it off right away and save 10% on your purchase today!" No, thanks. "Are you sure? You could save $25.00 today!" Nope, I'm good. Because the temptation to buy now and pay later to appease our lust for instant gratification is the gateway to debt.

Debt is like a cancer. It silently grows, often unnoticed, until it's too late.

Truly, I placed myself in that situation. I bought a house above my means. I financed a car that weighed me down with a monthly payment and insurance costs. I opted to charge everything I wanted instead of saving the cash to buy it outright.

There was no one to blame but myself.

I was the architect of my own financial downfall by giving in to the allure of instant gratification that clouded my judgment, always choosing pleasure over discipline. Each purchase on credit seemed like a small indulgence at the time, but collectively, they led to a mountain of debt towering over me.

The wake-up call came when I realized that my quality of life was suffering while drowning in debt and struggling to keep my head above water. I lived in a constant state of stress. Seeing my mentor living a life free of the burden of debt was a sobering moment of reckoning for me. His effortless ease and financial freedom served as a stark contrast to my own struggles. He felt no stress, no crushing pressure, and had the power to spend his money as he wished. It forced me to confront the harsh reality of my situation and come to terms with the consequences of my actions.

It was time to make some changes, starting with me.

It all began with Dave Ramsey, the financial guru renowned for his straightforward and practical financial philosophy. Through his books, podcasts, and YouTube channel, I learned the importance of living within my means, budgeting effectively, and tackling debt head-on. Using his "Baby Steps" method, I saved up a $1,000 emergency fund, which provided a little safety net for unexpected expenses. It took a lot of mental strength and discipline not to run out and spend it, but I persisted, and it was humbling to have it available when I needed it for a car repair. Subsequent steps involved aggressively paying off debts, building a fully funded emergency fund, investing in my future, leading to the goal of paying off my mortgage, and ultimately, building wealth and giving generously. The key lies in the deliberate and sequential nature of these steps.

Implementing Ramsey's plan demanded discipline and total commitment. I couldn't work longer than my scheduled shifts at work, so I opted to create an additional revenue source. Weekends were opportunities for extra work, while I decluttered my life by selling unnecessary things and curbed frivolous spending. With my sights set firmly on making money and paying debt, I finally began to see progress. Today, I am proud to declare that I'm abundantly debt-free, and with every fiber of my being, I resolve never to find myself in that disgraceful situation again.

Central to this financial philosophy and the true secret sauce is the concept of *delayed gratification*. It's the ability to defer immediate desires for long-term goals. Rather than giving in to the temptation of immediate rewards, you prioritize future benefits over present pleasures.

Simply said, put it back on the shelf and step away.

Instead, use a deliberate and calculated approach to decision-making. Do you really need that subscription? Can you make your iced coffee at home? Is that overpriced brand-name sweatshirt really going to make you feel more successful? Are there luxuries you can temporarily forego to pave the way for a future where you won't have to worry about sacrificing them?

Practicing delayed gratification empowers you to make strong-minded choices that align with your long-term goals. It's the sacrifices you make today that will ultimately lead to greater fulfillment and success in the future.

Consider the concept of an entrepreneur reinvesting profits back into their business instead of giving in to the temptation of immediate personal luxuries. A first-time millionaire doesn't run out and buy a Ferrari or a yacht. They turn around and reinvest it in something that will continue to make them money. The prerogative that wealthy individuals can spend money on whatever they want is not entirely true. They must continue to prioritize their spending and investments wisely to sustain their wealth over time.

One aspect of personal finance that is often neglected is the practice of maintaining a budget and understanding where every penny earned and spent is allocated. Every penny has a designated purpose, whether it's for bills, savings, or debt repayment. Maintaining a budget gives us full visibility and control over our finances, which helps us make informed decisions and effectively prioritize our spending. How many of us truly monitor our expenses? The simple act of tracking our pennies can help us steer clear of overspending.

Financial freedom is truly liberating. It's not about amassing wealth; rather, it's about controlling our finances and spending habits. Financial freedom is having the confidence to say "no" to those in-store credit card offers, no matter how sweet they try to make the deal. It's the ability to enjoy what you've got instead of wanting more. The sheer pleasure of watching your bank account grow as a result of your patience is a uniquely satisfying feeling. After all, fiscal responsibility over instant gratification is empowerment itself.

THE SUCCESS CHALLENGE #6

1. Create a budget as soon as possible. Begin by assessing your current financial situation, including income, expenses, debts, and savings. Determine your financial goals, whether it's debt repayment, saving for a specific purchase, or building an emergency fund. Allocate specific amounts for each expense category, ensuring that your income exceeds your expenses. Track your spending regularly to stay within your budget and adjust as needed.

2. Identify areas of your life where you indulge in impulsive spending or instant gratification. Challenge yourself to delay these expenditures. Before making a purchase, ask yourself if it aligns with your long-term financial goals and if it's worth sacrificing future financial security. Practice saying "no" to impulse buys and focus on prioritizing your financial well-being.

3. Set a goal to build an emergency fund to cover unexpected expenses and financial emergencies,

and determine an initial target amount, such as three to six months' worth of living expenses. Begin canceling unnecessary subscriptions and allocate the money toward your emergency fund. Then, set aside a small portion of your income each month into a dedicated savings account. Automate this process to ensure consistency. This step alone will save you years of hardships by preparing you for unexpected expenses.

"Choosing how to spend your time is life's greatest freedom."

—PROJECT LIFE MASTERY

Chapter Seven

TIME FREEDOM

THE ONLY THING more valuable than money is time. It's limited, and it's often wasted. True success for me is having freedom of both things—time and money—since they provide the most opportunities to enjoy life genuinely.

It's hard to have one but not the other.

Excessive wealth can lead to a life consumed by work, while a lack of financial stability can breed stress and uncertainty. And as politely as I can phrase this, there's no true joy in the stress of being broke.

The trick to balancing time and money is to establish multiple streams of passive income and structure your business to operate smoothly and build profits even in your absence. Occasionally, you can step in and push the metaphoric wheel to keep things running efficiently, then step back to watch it go.

Time freedom goes hand in hand with financial freedom. It's a fusion of the two that creates the gateway to a life where you call the shots. The utter freedom to spend your days as you please, unburdened by financial concerns, is nothing short of euphoric. Time freedom is more valuable than any possession because it gives you control over your most precious resource—your life. Possessions can be replaced, but time once spent is gone forever. Having the autonomy to decide how you spend each moment, pursuing your passions, investing in your relationships, and nurturing your well-being is the ultimate luxury. Living life on your terms, savoring every moment, and making the most out of the time you have is what any entrepreneur strives for.

Time freedom.

I wish I had known this years ago because there are so many unique ways to generate income that I hadn't thought to explore. Essentially, you can either sell a product or offer a service. Either way, establishing your own business is key. Starting a business opens opportunities to create multiple income streams and leverage your skills in a way that a traditional job might not allow.

One significant advantage of running your own business is the potential for tax benefits not available for personal use. Business owners can optimize their tax situation by utilizing the available deductions. Also, owning a business offers the opportunity to build equity and create long-term financial security. You can also enjoy full control over your work-life balance, allowing you to prioritize your time more effectively.

Once you've researched the steps to form a business in your state, you can develop a plan to turn your idea into a profitable venture: identify a product or service that addresses a specific need or solves a problem. Conduct market research to understand your target audience and the competitive landscape, which will help you refine your offering and position it effectively.

Next, create a more detailed business plan outlining your goals, strategies, and financial projections. Build a strong brand and a message that resonates with your audience, utilizing social media and marketing channels to promote your business to reach potential customers.

As you start to generate revenue, focus on managing your finances while exploring ways to grow the business. Reinvest profits into growing your business, and when possible, hire skilled employees who can help you scale operations and maintain high-quality products or services.

Finally, continue scaling your business and hiring someone to take over your role, allowing you to step back. With your newfound time freedom, you can focus on building another venture while your current business operates independently. You'll have the flexibility to step in and support your team when needed, exemplifying the qualities of a strong and effective leader.

This method is boiled down to the very basic essentials just to convey my point. Starting and running a business involves many moving parts, which vary based on your product or service. Still, the key takeaway is that establishing your own business raises the ceiling of income opportunities that may not be available with a regular job. This approach allows you to explore various avenues for generating income, tapping into markets that a traditional job won't offer. By creating a business, you can diversify your income streams and tailor it to your skillset.

Let's explore the idea that you should only spend money on things that will make you money and grant you time freedom. An example of this is investing in tools and equipment for a service-based business. For instance, if you start a landscaping business, purchasing lawnmowers, trimmers, and trailers to haul them will generate revenue each time they're used. The same idea goes for construction equipment, or any tools specific to your trade. On a large scale, purchasing an excavator might be expensive up front, but if someone contracts your excavation business for a construction project, then your excavator will eventually generate enough income to pay for itself and a second one to add to the fleet. With two excavators working, your revenue doubles, allowing you to purchase a third machine even faster. As you scale your business, your assets and revenue grow accordingly. Not to mention, the tax benefits associated with the depreciation of the equipment can further benefit your financial position. Once your excavator has generated enough income to afford an operator, you can pay them a generous wage while using the remaining revenue for reinvestments.

This principle remains the same across various fields. By strategically spending money on things that enhance your business's productivity and profitability, you not only increase your income potential but also free up your time. The more efficiently your business operates, the more time you have to focus on other endeavors.

To be successful in any venture, you absorb a substantial amount of risk. In many cases, the risk can be enough to cripple your business should something go wrong, as the business owner bears the weight of responsibility for the outcome. It may not feel like freedom at first, given the calculated risks and countless hours poured into the business startup. But that's exactly what sets successful entrepreneurs apart. If you're willing to roll up your sleeves and do whatever is necessary to secure your future time freedom, then the dedication to 18-hour days, 7 days a week is worth it.

Many people are satisfied with working a traditional job, and that's okay, too. It means their definition of success differs from others, and their purpose is valuable to business owners and vice versa. Their time freedom is limited to their work schedule and their financial status, but in the grand scheme of things, each role contributes to the overall functioning and success of an organization, and it's important to recognize and appreciate the diverse paths people take to find fulfillment and purpose in their work.

However, for the sake of *The Success Challenge*, I wish you unlimited time freedom. Time is so valuable that you should strive higher and refuse to settle. Take the leap and start your own business, diving into ventures that seem daunting to many. It will be challenging, but the reward—both in financial security and the priceless gift of time freedom—will be worth every effort. I challenge you to do whatever is necessary to create the life you desire, where you have both the time and money to live fully and freely.

THE SUCCESS CHALLENGE #7

1. Reflect on how you currently spend your time. Envision your perfect day unburdened by constraints. What activities would fill 24 hours in your average day? How would you balance work, leisure, and personal pursuits?

2. Pinpoint habits or routines that drain your time without significant returns. Recognizing these habits is crucial to reclaiming your time, whether it's excessive social media scrolling, procrastination, or other unproductive patterns.

3. Create a schedule that sustains productivity as you work toward your goal deadlines. Replace non-productive activities with tasks that enhance your financial, physical, and mental well-being.

4. Begin brainstorming business opportunities that align with your skills and market demand. Craft a business plan outlining your goals and strategies. Research your state's requirements for starting a business, including licenses, permits, and regulations. Once you feel prepared, take that first step towards entrepreneurship.

" *80% of success is just showing up.* "

—WOODY ALLEN

Chapter Eight

SHOW UP! ALL DAY, EVERY DAY

>————————<

MOTIVATION IS FLEETING. It's here one day and gone the next, only to return when the conditions are just right. The problem with relying solely on motivation to accomplish big things is its unpredictability. It's like a fair-weather friend who shows up when times are good but disappears when the going gets tough.

You know that surge of energy that comes from being motivated? It's an exhilarating feeling that makes everything seem possible, driven by the anticipation of achieving our desired outcome. We envision ourselves at the finish line, and that vision is the fuel to the motivational fire. You start the day excited and full of ideas, eager to tackle your goals. But what happens when you wake up in a bad mood or face a setback? Suddenly, that spark of motivation is nowhere to be found, doused by the negative emotions clouding our minds. Those exciting tasks now feel intimidating, monumental, and far away.

As Woody Allen famously said, "80% of success is just showing up." In essence, that's all there is to it. Showing up and working on your goals is the only way to make progress. Many people quit when they feel pressure or discomfort. They don't force themselves to sit down, stand up, or get moving. They prioritize comfort over achievement and quit.

Discipline and consistency are what keep the momentum going. Motivation provides a powerful initial push, but it's self-discipline that keeps you moving forward when the excitement fades. Have the discipline to show up *every day* and put in the necessary work, regardless of how you feel. Through consistent work, we establish habits and routines that support our goals so that progress becomes a part of our daily lives.

You won't see the results right away, but keep showing up. Slowly, steadily, consistently.

But what if you're too tired and would rather spend time relaxing? *Keep showing up.* What if you're upset, had a bad day, and can't focus? *Keep showing up.* What if you're not seeing any results and you're feeling discouraged? *Keep showing up!*

People don't make it because they quit. They say they've tried everything *except* showing up every day. Success comes to those who don't quit, and they show up no matter the conditions. It's difficult, yes. But we all have this incredible power within our minds to make ourselves do it.

Developing self-discipline starts with setting clear, achievable goals, as we discussed earlier when developing your actionable plan. Once your goals are defined, break them down into smaller, manageable tasks. This makes it easier to stay on track and see progress regularly.

There are several methods to try to discover which best suits your level of comfort and focus. For example, the Pomodoro technique involves breaking your work into intervals, typically 25 minutes long, separated by short breaks. Or the "Don't Break the Chain" method, which is setting a daily goal and marking each day you successfully complete on a calendar. The visual reminder of your progress can be highly motivating.

Time blocking is an effective technique for dedicating time periods to certain activities. It allows you to guide yourself through your day with a structured schedule of tasks and allocated time slots. By planning your tasks in advance, you eliminate the need to constantly decide what to work on next, conserving mental energy and enhancing productivity. Follow the schedule you've set for yourself, knowing that each block of time is dedicated to a specific task or objective, and don't allow yourself to become distracted.

Consistency is the practice of adhering to this plan day in and day out. It means committing to your tasks even when you are tired, stressed, or simply not in the mood. Making these tasks a non-negotiable part of your daily routine is crucial, so set aside a specific time each day dedicated to work and create an environment that supports your efforts.

I wanted to play the piano when I was six years old. My mom was very supportive, and I remember her asking me very clearly, "Is this really something that you want to do? Because once you're signed up for lessons, you're going to stick with it." She had wisely known that taking on new things, especially an instrument, would require practice and dedication, which, to a child, was especially challenging. I mean, how many 6-year-olds have the patience to sit still for a minute, let alone maintain a practice schedule?

I remember how thrilled I was to go to my first lesson. My music instructor was an older gentleman with years of experience as an accomplished pianist. He was very direct, rather dry, and incredibly strict.

After a weekly lesson, my job was to practice at home everything he had shown me. Not knowing how to do this, I stumbled through learning how to read the notes, the keys, and the chords while maintaining good posture and hand placement.

It was hard! And not much fun at all.

I plunked on the keys during the 20 minutes my mom required me to practice each day. While I didn't progress much at first, I had been building the habit of being consistent and dedicated. Even when I was having a bad day at school, it was no exception. Mom told me to sit down and practice.

And so, I did.

Within a year, I learned to play Mozart's Minuet in C Major, Allegro in B-Flat Major, and Andante in E-Flat Major. I had practiced and refined my skills enough to perform as background piano ambiance for an event held at the historic Davenport Hotel in Spokane, Washington, at the ripe age of seven.

Over the next several years, I performed classical scores at the Allied Arts Festival, earned gold medals in competitions, and played background Christmas music in the parlor at Spokane's historic Campbell House Museum on the Campbell's original piano. (An unforgettable honor!) The one thing that remained consistent was my dedication and consistency to practicing my piano every day. Had my mom allowed me to quit when it got difficult, or if she hadn't forced me to sit down and develop a habit of practice—no matter how much I whined and protested—I wouldn't have had the honor of these accomplishments.

Self-discipline and consistency have been present throughout my life, and they're the reason I've been able to experience such meaningful moments. Writing this book is a direct result of consistency. There were days that I stared at my cursor on a blank screen and others when I typed for hours.

I showed up. I didn't quit. And this book is the outcome.

Research shows that forming a new habit takes an average of 66 days. Conversely, breaking a habit can take anywhere from 18 to 254 days. The commitment required to change established routines is huge! But the payoff is worth it. Start with small, manageable changes and gradually increase your commitment. For example, if your goal is to exercise, begin by working out for 15 minutes each day and slowly increase the time as the habit becomes ingrained. Consistency in these small actions builds momentum over time, leading to significant progress.

Don't quit. Keep showing up.

Discipline requires a strong sense of self-awareness. Pay attention to what triggers procrastination or distraction and develop strategies to overcome these obstacles. This might involve setting stricter boundaries for your work time, learning to say no to non-essential tasks, or finding ways to stay motivated when enthusiasm disappears.

Don't quit. Keep showing up.

By prioritizing discipline and consistency over fleeting motivation and focusing on building habits, you establish a reliable framework for achieving your goals. It ensures that progress continues even when the excitement fades and discomfort sets in. Motivation is great, but momentum is what brings you results.

Don't quit.

Keep showing up.

THE SUCCESS CHALLENGE #8

1. Develop a habit-building plan. Outline the habits you want to build and create a 30-day plan to integrate these habits into your daily routine. Track your progress and stay committed to these habits until they become second nature. Make the commitment to show up every day, no matter what.

2. Look at your actionable plan and select your #1 prioritized goal. Create a structured schedule to accomplish the tasks that have been broken into smaller, manageable steps. Use methods like time blocking or the Pomodoro Technique to organize your tasks and maintain productivity.

3. Establish accountability measures. Share your goals and progress with a trusted friend, mentor, or accountability partner. Regularly update them on your achievements and setbacks. This external accountability reinforces your commitment and encourages consistent effort. Above all, keep showing up!

"There is nothing more beautiful than someone who goes out of their way to make life beautiful for others."

—MANDY HALE

Chapter Nine

COMMUNITY SUPPORT

>————————————<

THE INTERNET IS A GOLDMINE for anything you can possibly dream of. Many successful entrepreneurs rely on Google for answers to things they're unsure how to do, and I can vouch for that. We always have a resource at our disposal, and there is an answer to almost all of our questions. In addition to answers, more specifically, there is an online community of people who enjoy helping and sharing their stories.

When I decided to write a children's book and have it illustrated by a talented artist, I had no idea where to start. How much would it cost? How the heck do I find an illustrator? How do I put it all together? I started researching, and a Google search led me to a Facebook community group page called "Children's Book Authors & Illustrators and Marketing."

I joined the group of 40k members and started

poking around at the posts, absorbing what I could find and making a list of questions. There were so many artists and writers in that group, from beginners to advanced, and the wealth of knowledge was tremendous.

When I mustered up the courage to post a question to the group—a daunting thing for me as a self-described introvert—I asked the basic questions for illustrating a book, and the positive, helpful responses were nearly overwhelming! People shared their experiences, offered advice on pricing, and even recommended illustrators they had worked with. One member provided a step-by-step guide on how to approach an illustrator, what to include in a contract, and how to manage the project timeline. Another member directed me to resources for self-publishing and marketing the book once it was complete. I took detailed notes and began to feel a little more confident about the process.

I reached out to a few recommended illustrators, sharing my vision for the book and requesting quotes. Negotiating terms and discussing artistic direction was a new experience for me, but the support from the Facebook group gave me the confidence to move forward. Eventually, I found an illustrator whose style matched perfectly with the story I wanted to tell.

To this day, I continue to rely on the group for advice and feedback. From tips to strategies, the community was an invaluable resource. The tasks weren't always easy, and there were moments of doubt and frustration, but the positive encouragement from the group was instrumental in keeping me on track.

Accessing a group's collective experience has been a constant source of practical advice and moral support, and you can't put a price on that.

The melting pot within the internet is where individuals from diverse backgrounds, cultures, and experiences converge. I've found it particularly rewarding that accessing a variety of perspectives only enriches what we learn. Exposure to alternative viewpoints gives us a broader understanding of the world and challenges our preconceived notions, even when we don't exactly agree with all of them. But, by engaging with people from different walks of life, we expand our horizons by learning from those who have lived unique experiences and share their insights so that we can use these perspective shifts as a stepping stone in our work.

Anyone can access online courses and workshops to develop skills and learn independently. A simple online search will provide you with countless opportunities to choose courses tailored to your interests, goals, and areas of expertise.

Before the internet, the chances of attending an Ivy League school were a distant dream because of barriers such as location and tuition costs. Now, with the rise of online education, this idea has changed, giving access to the most prestigious institutions. This presents a great opportunity for the average person to pursue their goals without traditional barriers. It's the very reason I got certified by Harvard Business School Online after taking the Entrepreneurship Essentials course.

There's something for everyone, from business and entrepreneurship to creative arts, technology, personal development, and beyond. Leverage these online courses and workshops and acquire new skills, expand your base with community support, and gather the resources you need for success. The opportunities are truly endless in the digital realm.

THE SUCCESS CHALLENGE #9

1. Do an online search on Google and Facebook to identify groups or forums aligned with your interests. Establish connections in the groups and read through the archive of questions and answers to orient yourself in the groups.

2. Attend virtual and in-person meetups, webinars, workshops, or networking events within your industry or field of interest. Connect and network with like-minded individuals, exchange ideas, and build relationships that can offer support along the way.

"*Once you've accepted your flaws, no one can use them against you.*"

—UNKNOWN

Chapter Ten

EMBRACE YOUR FLAWS

›————————‹

IF THERE'S ONE thing I wish I could go back and tell my younger self, it would be to love myself a little more for who I *am* and not focus on who I am *not*.

It all started in the sixth grade. Unbearable acne, awkward, gangly arms and legs, big feet, crooked teeth, and frizzy hair. To top it off, 99% of my t-shirts had an image of a horse on them. Every elementary school has that one weird girl who is obsessed with horses.

That was me. Cringe.

My mom wasn't into fashion, and she believed that whatever was popular or in style was "just a fad." If that's what all the "cool kids" were wearing—brand names and virtually anything from the late '90s and early '2000s—I was not allowed to. So, I wore my mom's high-waisted Wrangler jeans, the farthest thing from a trendy kind of girl. I understand what my mom was trying to teach me by not allowing me to follow the trends; she wanted me to become my own person and not be influenced by popularity. But wow, it was a struggle and a huge blow to my self-esteem, as I constantly felt out of place and disconnected from my peers.

And I struggled for a very long time.

My low self-esteem and insecurities followed me throughout middle school and high school. Even though I had grown out of my awkward appearance phase, I never felt like I would fit in with any crowd because of my internalized beliefs, and my confidence level was so low that I found every excuse not to speak in front of groups of people. I was painfully reserved and focused my attention on schoolwork and escaping to the worlds within novels rather than socializing.

When it was time for me to get a job, I knew I had to force myself outside of my comfort zone. Some of my friends had gotten hired at a local McDonald's, and I decided to give it a try.

Soft-spoken, timid, and terribly shy, I managed to get through my interview and was hired on the spot. I collected my uniform and started training the next day.

My reserved nature and lack of confidence proved to be a significant obstacle during that first day.

Interacting with customers and handling the fast-paced environment was beyond overwhelming. I strained to assert myself, and my anxiety was through the roof.

After that first day, I knew deep down that I had to embrace discomfort if I wanted to meet the job expectations. I discovered that nobody cared about my appearance; they just wanted their orders taken.

Over the weeks, I learned to project my voice confidently, call out orders, greet every customer warmly, and handle interactions with those who were upset or dissatisfied. Surprisingly, I became quite comfortable in my role and seemed to be growing into a completely different person.

Reflecting on why this happened so quickly, I realized that when I stopped worrying about my imperfections and stopped concerning myself with my appearance, I pushed through a metaphorical wall—a wall that I had placed there and reinforced with negative thought patterns about myself.

It was all made up in my head.

In fact, cute customers and co-workers flirted with me, and I was often asked to give out my phone number when working the drive-through window.

That wall in my mind was finally torn down. I

embraced the fact that I was meant to be this way, and my imperfections didn't define my worth.

Nobody cares about my flaws, and nobody cares about *your* flaws.

My self-perception had been hindering my opportunities to step outside of my comfort zone and present myself as a confident young woman. It wasn't until I grew older that I truly understood how profoundly our opinions of ourselves shape our realities.

We are what we think.

Our thoughts and beliefs about ourselves directly influence our actions, choices, and interactions with others. By shifting my focus to my strengths rather than my perceived flaws, I opened a world of possibilities and began to realize my full potential. True confidence comes from within, and it's our inner belief in ourselves that ultimately shapes our external experiences.

The way you speak to yourself matters. It becomes your identity, so be kind to yourself. Inside your mind, especially. Speak gently, as if you were talking to a special friend. Remind yourself of your strengths, accomplishments, and unique qualities. We often become our harshest critics, focusing on our shortcomings and mistakes, but this only erodes our self-esteem. Instead, practice self-compassion and acknowledge your efforts, even when things don't go as planned. Celebrate your victories, no matter how small they may seem.

When negative thoughts arise, counter them with positive affirmations. Replace "I can't" with "I *will*" and "I'm not good enough" with "I *am* capable and worthy." A simple mental shift like this can transform your outlook and empower you to tackle challenges with a renewed sense of determination. Over time, these positive affirmations become ingrained in your mindset, helping you to build an optimistic attitude toward life.

We have the remarkable ability to influence our experiences with an adjustment in perception. A perfect example is the transformation of nervousness into excitement. When we feel nervous jitters and sweaty palms, we can command ourselves to believe that we're not nervous. We are excited! By reframing nervous energy as excitement, we can channel our emotions into a positive force. This potential to "trick" our minds into believing empowering perspectives can help us overcome fears that we wouldn't dare to face. A mental shift impacts our performance, and we can push through challenges with a little thought.

When we internalize limiting beliefs and doubt our abilities, we set the stage for our own underachievement. These beliefs shape our perceptions, behaviors, and choices, creating a self-perpetuating cycle of mediocrity. If we convince ourselves that we're incapable of doing something, we subconsciously sabotage our efforts, avoid taking necessary risks, and thereby solidify our failure.

A profound revelation I learned from my childhood is that our actions are parallel with our beliefs, which reinforces the notion that we are inadequate. In turn, this emphasizes the limiting belief, making it even more difficult to break free from its grip and fulfill our true potential. If only I had known how special I was back then, I could have fully enjoyed my childhood experiences and lived in the moment instead of hiding behind my insecurities. The pain I put myself through was not necessary, and my inner child has finally accepted this truth.

Flaws are not signs of inadequacy. Admitting vulnerability as a strength rather than a weakness becomes a transformative paradigm shift. Accepting our flaws nurtures authenticity, which is something to be most proud of. *Love yourself just as you are.*

THE SUCCESS CHALLENGE #10

1. Pay attention to the language you use when describing yourself or your abilities. Whenever you catch yourself engaging in negative self-talk or self-criticism, pause and challenge those thoughts. Ask yourself if there's evidence to support these beliefs or if they're old patterns of thinking. Reframe negative statements into more neutral or positive affirmations that acknowledge your flaws without attaching judgment or self-doubt.

2. Purposefully put yourself in situations where you feel vulnerable about a particular flaw. For instance, if you're self-conscious about your public speaking skills, volunteer to speak at a small event or meeting. Embrace the discomfort as an opportunity for growth and break down that metaphorical self-limiting wall. Celebrate the feeling of accomplishment when you're finished and associate positive feelings with that action.

"Confidence is not:
They will like me.
Confidence is:
I'll be fine if they don't."

—CHRISTINA GRIMMIE

Chapter Eleven

CONFIDENCE WILL MOVE MOUNTAINS

>———————————<

AS MITOCHONDRIA ARE the powerhouse of a cell, confidence is the powerhouse of success. While that silly tidbit from school might seem trivial, I found it a fantastic analogy for the significance of what self-confidence can do for us. Just as mitochondria generate the energy required for cells to function, confidence fuels our ability to take decisive actions.

Confidence is our *intent*.

It's walking into a room and shifting the energy. Without saying a word, we can either command attention and respect, or blend into the background shadows of insecurity. Confidence influences how others perceive and respond to you. People are naturally drawn to confident individuals, seeing them as more competent and trustworthy, whereas confidence-lacking people give off a vibe of "please don't talk to me" and "go away."

Throughout my career, I've had the privilege of interacting with a diverse array of individuals, each with their unique personalities. Through conversations, it became clear that those who confidently made eye contact, were open, and engaged in friendly chats tended to be more successful. On the contrary, people who were more reserved, struggled with eye contact, and shied away from making connections seemed to fade into the background.

My experience working at an assisted living facility at the front desk was a place to witness this firsthand. Throughout the day, I would encounter marketing representatives from the industry stopping by to drop off promotional materials and literature to advertise their services. Some would approach my desk with a timid demeanor, quickly deliver the items, and leave with a few generic words exchanged. In contrast, others took the time to visit with me, asking questions and showing genuine interest. I noticed that those who lingered and chatted with me left a lasting impression. Those who ducked out as soon as they handed me their information became a passing thought. When it came time to consider hiring services, it was the confident ones who had taken the time to connect with me that stood out and ultimately received my call.

The key difference between the two types of marketers was, of course, *confidence*.

Another striking example of the impact of confidence can be observed through a change in management at a local business. Following its acquisition by new owners, the business underwent minimal changes apart from the signage announcing the transition.

However, despite this change, there was a noticeable decline in business. Loyal customers drifted away, and significant commercial accounts took their business elsewhere. The once-prosperous venture slipped backward, tarnishing its reputation in the process.

While it's expected that new owners may lack experience at first, the main problem affecting the business was a clear lack of confidence to put themselves out there and engage.

As customer loss increased, it became crucial for the business to actively reach out to the community. They required a strategy to establish themselves as the top choice and put in a relentless effort to reclaim prominence in their customers' minds. It was essential to build a rapport and network with those commercial accounts they had lost and win their trust back. They should have left no stone unturned in their efforts to revive the business.

The new owners lacked confidence in their *ability* to do the job. Not only did they hinder their progress by hesitating and avoiding, but they also undermined their own potential for building wealth. It was a devastating loss that could have been reversed with some confidence.

Believing in yourself and your abilities empowers you to make bold decisions and approach challenges from a position of strength. It's the driving force behind seeing things differently, which is necessary when looking for solutions to setbacks.

Dr. Jordan Peterson, a clinical psychologist, offers a nuanced perspective on confidence that I've found to be quite valuable. In his lectures, he emphasizes the connection between self-confidence and personal responsibility, arguing that taking ownership of our lives and our actions is essential for building self-assurance. It's a complex idea, but he's saying that we must claim responsibility for our current situation.

It's by choice that we suffer or celebrate.

Once we accept responsibility, rather than wallow in self-pity or blame everyone else for the obstacles, we can make adjustments to confront challenges head-on. Dr. Peterson claims that individuals willing to confront their fears and accept their failures are more likely to develop a strong sense of confidence.

Feeling good is important, but believing in your ability to tackle anything and seize opportunities is essential to success. When you have confidence in your ability to succeed, you're more inclined to take risks and pursue new ventures. This confident mindset is what fuels progress.

Personal growth doesn't happen overnight. It took me *years* to build my confidence, and it's still an ongoing feat. The process of building confidence is like training a muscle. It requires consistent effort, patience, and self-reflection. I constantly work at it and place myself in situations where I will grow. They start out as stressful and intimidating, but once I show up with the intent to be confident, I'm a force to be reckoned with.

Confidence comes from authenticity, as it earns respect from others. People can sense when you are genuine, and this confidence creates a lasting impression. So, keep pushing your boundaries and just be yourself. Your commitment to growth and self-belief will make you unstoppable.

THE SUCCESS CHALLENGE #11

1. Actively seek constructive criticism from mentors, peers, or trusted individuals in your field. Use feedback to identify areas for improvement and take intentional steps to address them. Remember to view failure as a natural part of the learning process rather than a reflection of your abilities. Analyze setbacks objectively and always be accountable. Your confidence will grow by processing and applying this information to your continuous development.

2. Take time to reflect on your experiences and interactions, considering instances where you may have struggled or felt less confident. Once you've identified areas for improvement, create a plan outlining specific steps to address these weaknesses. This might involve seeking additional training or education, practicing new skills, seeking guidance from mentors or peers, or participating in an event that places you in a position that will require you to face your fears and build confidence.

"*Work hard in silence,
let success be your noise.*"

—FRANK OCEAN

Chapter Twelve

THE REWARD SYSTEM

>———————<

A LITTLE REWARD can make a huge difference along the way. The path to our goals is a long one, and I firmly believe in the power of celebrating personal triumphs to keep us motivated.

There's a fascinating psychology associated with the reward system and our mindset. When we receive a reward, whether a physical product or intangible like acknowledgment, our brain releases dopamine, a neurotransmitter associated with pleasure and motivation. This surge of dopamine reinforces the behavior that led to the reward and creates a positive association with our efforts, making us more inclined to repeat them in the future.

That's a pretty good reason to treat yo' self when you're winning!

When I set out to write this book, I knew it would be difficult to manage between raising 4 children and running several businesses with my husband. Writing is my passion, so I created the space and prioritized time after everyone went to bed to stay up and write. Knowing it would be challenging, I wanted to make the experience fun and something I'd look forward to each night. I decided to incorporate small rewards for accomplishing each task along the way.

The process began with brainstorming and outlining my book. After completing the initial outline, I treated myself to a new set of high-quality pens and a beautiful notebook. This way, I'm celebrating my progress and gaining practical tools to help me continue my work with enthusiasm.

As I moved on to writing the first few chapters, I set smaller, more frequent rewards. For example, after finishing a particularly difficult chapter, I allowed myself an hour to enjoy my favorite TV show guilt-free. These little breaks provided a much-needed mental refresh and made the writing process more enjoyable.

Editing was one of the most arduous parts of the writing journey. To make it more manageable, I broke it down into sections and rewarded myself after each section was thoroughly reviewed. A fresh cup of coffee or a 30-minute break to scroll through Instagram became my go-to reward. Mixing the editing process with these fun little treats made it less daunting and provided much-needed mental breaks.

When I finally completed the first draft of my book, I celebrated with a special dinner with my family at my favorite restaurant. This was a significant milestone and acknowledging it with a meaningful reward reinforced the sense of achievement and motivated me to start on the next one right away.

Throughout the entire process, these small rewards played a crucial role in maintaining my momentum. Each reward—or mental break—helped to create a positive association with my writing efforts, making the process more fulfilling and enjoyable. By celebrating each accomplishment, I was able to stay inspired and committed to my goal, ultimately leading to the successful completion of my book.

Incorporating small rewards into your routine is a powerful strategy. However, while rewarding yourself for accomplishments can be a powerful motivator, it's important to be cautious of slipping into self-indulgence. This can happen when you begin to feel entitled to a reward for every small task you complete. Such a mindset can lead to an imbalance, where the focus shifts from genuine productivity to merely seeking gratification. To avoid this pitfall, ensure your rewards are proportionate to the effort expended and serve to genuinely enhance your motivation rather than becoming mere distractions. Balance is crucial; use rewards to boost your productivity, not as an excuse for complacency.

Each milestone represents progress and deserves acknowledgment. Create that positive feedback loop in your mind and nurture a positive attitude toward a challenging goal. So, go ahead and celebrate your achievements, both big and small, and keep pushing your boundaries.

THE SUCCESS CHALLENGE #12

1. Identify your main goal and divide it into incremental milestones. For example, if your goal is to exercise daily, set milestones such as consistently working out for one week. Assign rewards that match the effort required for each milestone. A small reward, like a bubble bath, can be given for daily exercise achievements, and a larger reward, like a night out with friends, can be reserved for significant milestones, such as maintaining your workout regime for a month.

2. Create a list of enjoyable and beneficial rewards. After reaching a milestone, reward yourself with activities promoting relaxation and happiness, such as a movie night, a nature walk, or a hobby. Avoid counterproductive rewards that might undermine your efforts, like unhealthy snacks or excessive screen time. Proportional rewards make the accomplishments feel meaningful.

"One thing we all need to realize — the fear is in your mind. The fear is what we have created. If we created it, we have the antidote to destroy it!"

—DAVID GOGGINS

Chapter Thirteen

MANAGING FEAR

>———————————<

FEAR IS INEVITIBLE. If you look at someone presenting during an event, a new employee on their first day on the job, or an aspiring entrepreneur about to launch their first business, fear is a universal experience. The key difference between those who succeed and those who don't often lies in how they manage and harness their fear.

You will inevitably face fear in various forms. Fear of failure, fear of rejection, and fear of the unknown... Understanding and managing this fear can help you to get past it. It's a natural response to perceived threats. It activates the body's "fight or flight" response, releasing adrenaline and other stress hormones. This response can be traced back to our evolutionary past, where physical threats required immediate and decisive action. However, in the context of modern-day entrepreneurship, these threats are more psychological than physical.

Fear is not the task itself. Rather, it's the feeling that comes up when you're about to do it. An emotional wall is thrown up to stop you from going forward. Our minds dislike pain, so they invent thoughts to divert you from the task and feelings to defer you from the action. You'll remain there, stuck but safe in your comfort zone. Discontent and miserable but secure. Rather than circumvent, you must go through this emotional wall. Notice, name, and face the thoughts and feelings that show up. Accept and diffuse them by looking at them, not running away. Do what matters by connecting your values and reminding yourself why they are important. Although it may be painful, push through. Because on the other side of this emotional wall, you'll find what you're looking for.

Psychologists like Dr. Susan Jeffers, author of *Feel the Fear and Do It Anyway,* argue that fear should not be eliminated but *embraced.* She explains that by confronting our fears, we can reduce their power over us. This concept is rooted in cognitive-behavioral therapy (CBT), which suggests that changing our thoughts about fear can change our feelings and behaviors. To better understand this, let's break it down:

First, instead of trying to avoid or get rid of fear, we should accept it as part of life. Fear is a metaphoric animal within all of us that cannot be eliminated. We can put it on a leash and teach it how to be managed rather than letting it control us.

Next, we confront it. When we face our fears, we expose ourselves to the situations that trigger those fears. This process is known as exposure therapy in the realm of CBT. By gradually and repeatedly facing our fears in controlled settings, we become desensitized to them. This means that the more we confront our fears, the less intimidating they become over time. For example, if you have a fear of public speaking, practicing speaking in front of small groups can gradually reduce your anxiety.

CBT is based on the idea that our thoughts influence our feelings and behaviors. We will become the very thoughts that we think. If we change the way we think about a fear-inducing situation, we can alter our emotional and behavioral responses to it. For instance, if you think, "I will fail and embarrass myself," your fear will increase. CBT encourages replacing these negative thoughts with more positive and realistic ones, like "I'm prepared, I'm confident, and I can handle this." By changing our thoughts about fear and confronting it, we diminish its power over us. When we see fear as something in a different light, it loses its ability to paralyze us. We hold the end of the leash on the metaphoric beast.

I remember when I had to give a presentation to my class. It wasn't just any presentation, either. It was a massive end-of-the-year senior culminating project that would determine my final grades for the year.

The topic was about my experience volunteering 20 hours at the Women's and Children's Free Restaurant in the basement of a local church. The project itself was fun! I met many wonderful people and served dinner to those in need.

But, when the day came that I was to present my slideshow, I was an absolute nervous wreck. Sweaty palms, fluttering heart, and a fear response that fought against me to run away as quickly as possible.

I stumbled through the first part of the presentation, my voice shaking and my mind blanking out. It felt as if the walls were closing in on me. Then, I got an idea. Knowing that I had no problem sitting at my desk and talking to my classmates, I imagined myself sitting at my desk, having a casual conversation about my volunteer experience with just my classmate who sat across from me. I imagined that everyone else was busy chatting amongst themselves and not paying attention to me.

This mental shift actually worked!

My nerves began to calm, and I slowed down and started speaking more confidently and clearly. I focused on my classmates' encouraging nods, which helped me get through the rest of the presentation smoothly.

By the end of my slideshow, I felt a rushing sense of triumph and utter relief. This trick got me through the presentation, and I passed the class with flying colors. I had found a coping strategy and reduced my fear's power over me.

A more recent experience happened that didn't end up with the result I wanted, but I found success by pushing through my self-limitation and changing the internal narrative about my ability to speak publicly.

I attended a writer's conference with high hopes of pitching my fiction manuscript to an agent and securing a contract. Fully prepared and practiced, I stepped into the event auditorium and immediately felt the fear response trigger.

Frustrated with myself, I tried to rein in my

thoughts and smother them with affirmations. But, my emotional response to the fear was overwhelming. As I nervously took my place in line, I was acutely aware of the hum of conversation at each of the agent's tables, which were lined up across the room. The gaze of everyone in line felt heavy on me, and the agents appeared intimidating.

I wanted to do this more than anything. Even if I didn't succeed this time, I was determined to learn from the experience so I could come back better prepared next time.

Glancing at my watch, I had time to escape the room and collect myself. I strode to the bathroom, and thankfully, it was empty. As cliché and corny as it may sound, I stared at myself in the mirror and began quietly chanting, "You're okay. You got this."

With each repetition, I felt a small surge of confidence. Or maybe it was adrenaline? Either way, I knew that if I could just get through this, I would be stronger for it. After a few minutes, I took a deep breath and returned to the room, feeling a newfound sense of calm. I had put my metaphoric fear-beast back on a leash, this time controlled and subdued.

As I stepped back into line, the agents seemed a

little less intimidating, and the chatter of the room faded into the background. The affirmations helped me center myself, and I felt more prepared to face the challenge ahead. It wasn't about perfection; it was about progress and pushing through my fears. I was ready to give it my best shot, knowing that whatever the outcome, I had already succeeded by simply showing up and trying again.

When it was my turn, I stepped up to the agent's table and took a seat. She tapped on the timer, and it began counting down from five minutes.

I introduced myself and launched into my pitch. No sooner than I got my first sentence out, she sat up and said, "Stop! You lost me. You said it was a Young Adult novel, but your main character is too old to be in that genre."

At that moment, my heart sank, and I felt the familiar grip of fear tightening around me. But I smiled and took a deep breath, remembering the confidence I had built up just moments before. Instead of crumbling under the critique, I decided to engage and learn from the feedback. I calmly asked for her insights on how I could adjust my pitch to better fit the Young Adult genre.

Her response was surprisingly helpful. She

provided some valuable tips on how to align my story with the genre's expectations, and we casually chatted until the timer went off. Although the initial rejection stung, it was all a part of the learning process.

After the session, I thanked her for her time and advice, feeling a mix of disappointment and determination. I had faced my fear and learned from the experience, which was a victory in itself. This meeting reinforced the importance of pushing through self-imposed limits and embracing the growth that comes from facing challenges head-on. I knew that with these new insights, I would refine my pitch and come back stronger and fearless the next time.

We're all fearful when facing unfamiliar things. And we're normal humans for it, too. The important thing to remember about fear is to embrace it and not run from it. Push through the emotional wall! And remember, even the most seasoned professionals experience fear.

You've got to manage it before it manages you.

THE SUCCESS CHALLENGE #13

1. Practice calming your nervous system. Set aside 10-15 minutes each day for mindfulness meditation. Find a quiet space, sit comfortably, and focus on your breath. Inhale deeply through your nose, hold for a few seconds, and exhale slowly through your mouth. As you breathe, pay attention to the sensations in your body and let go of any tension. Apps like Headspace and Calm can guide you through mindfulness practices. Mindfulness and deep breathing can reduce the physiological symptoms of fear by calming the nervous system.

2. When you notice a fear-inducing thought, pause and examine its validity. Challenge negative assumptions by asking yourself questions like, "Is this thought based on facts or assumptions?" and "What is the worst that could happen, and how likely is it?" Replace negative thoughts with more balanced and positive ones. Change "I can't do this" to "I can handle this step by step."

"It's only by saying
_NO_ that you can concentrate
on the things that are
really important."

—STEVE JOBS

Chapter Fourteen

THE POWER OF SAYING NO

IF THERE'S ONE lesson I wish I'd learned a lot sooner, it's knowing that I am allowed to say "no." It's rather confusing because we're raised to step outside our comfort zone and say "yes!" to things, as it opens doors and creates bigger and better opportunities. While this is true, we must also understand the equal importance of saying no.

My toxic trait is saying yes to everyone who asks me for help. I have an automatic obligation to make them feel better or to help them accomplish their task, no matter the cost. It's gotten me into some stressful situations that required significant effort and time to resolve, and the memory of those experiences still haunts me. I had no comprehension of what a personal boundary was, and it set me back from accomplishing my own goals because my already limited time was absorbed by helping others.

Recently, my schedule cleared, and I felt inspired to take on more personal projects. I was a bundle of excitement because I had the right tools and mindset to make it happen, and I was going to become even more successful by finishing these projects.

I started out with a bang, jumping out of bed every morning to get an early start and cranking out productivity. But, as the weeks went on, the requests for my help began to pile up. One person needed my assistance with their project, then another asked me to take on a task. An email seeking guidance arrived, followed by another phone call, and then yet another visitor seeking my time and energy.

My motivation ground to a halt and my personal productivity jammed like the cars on a freeway during rush hour.

I had heaped way too much on my plate, and I was desperately trying to keep up the momentum I had when I started. Sure, my mind was still focused on the outcome and results, and I was determined to keep my promises to myself, but my heart was struggling to maintain the workload that I had placed on my shoulders.

I prioritized everyone else's projects before mine to quickly get them finished and off my plate. Then, I began to feel annoyed and snippy when I had to get up from my computer to run an errand, or cook a meal for my family, or do anything that pulled me away from the projects. I didn't realize that these projects were sucking the energy out of me and turning my mindset into a negative space from the pressure and stress of trying to get it all done.

Even though I enjoyed helping people, I had forgotten to help myself. Pretty soon, my mindset took a nosedive, and I turned on myself.

I couldn't do anything right in my own eyes. My thoughts were counterproductive and negative. I gained a few pounds? *How could I let that happen?* I got behind in my writing schedule? *I should have stayed up later and got it done!* My submission to a magazine was rejected? *Why bother submitting anything if I didn't have the time to improve it?*

These thoughts were *horrible*. I was so mean to myself and had no reason to be that way. It was the stress talking. I was the one who put on that stress by failing to say "no," and I needed to be the one to take it off. That's when I made a promise to myself. I would only do the things that brought me joy. If I didn't like it, I wouldn't do it.

Now, I think it's fair to state the obvious: daily chores and adulting were exempt from my joy rule. But when someone reached out to ask for my help with their project, I would pause before responding to consider my workload and determine if I could spare the time to give them what they needed. If not, I would politely decline and offer to revisit in the future when my schedule would be more accommodating.

You must prioritize protecting your time, heart, and happiness. We all have twenty-four hours in a day, and it's up to you to decide how to spend that time. Don't let others take that precious time away from you unless you fully consent to give it.

It took a long time to get comfortable with rejection, but after a few tries, my strategy worked. To say no effectively, try to be polite yet firm. You are under no obligation to someone else, so if they ask for your time, you have every right to decline. More importantly, you don't owe them an explanation, so never feel compelled to provide one.

When I'm asked to do something I don't want to do, I simply thank them for the opportunity and tell them

I'm unable to take on another project/purchase this item/ go to this location/commit to this task at the moment. I often add that we can revisit this in the future when my schedule is more accommodating. This approach respects both your boundaries and the person making the request.

If it's something I don't want to revisit in the near future, I simply leave the conversation at "thank you, but no thank you" and carry on. As an empath, I can't stand the feeling of rejection, so I equally despise rejecting someone. However, after experiencing the stress of trying to please everyone, I realized that rejection is just a part of life. Everyone experiences it, and it's not inherently bad as long as it's done without malice.

If the individual is persistent and pushy, my responses become shorter. If they continue to fill my inbox after I've said "no, thank you," I don't hesitate to hit the block button faster than they can say, "would you be interested in..." This approach protects my time and energy, ensuring that I can focus on what truly matters to me.

Time is incredibly precious, and your future depends on how you choose to spend it. To achieve success and accomplish the goals that you set, it's essential to set boundaries and protect your time. Saying no to things that do not align with your priorities is not only a right but a necessary practice. Do this, and I assure you, you'll maintain focus on your goals and channel your energy into pursuits that truly matter to you. Establishing clear boundaries allows you to manage your time effectively and prevents you from being overwhelmed by unnecessary commitments.

Remember, every time you say yes to something that doesn't serve your goals, you are saying no to something that could. Be intentional with your time, prioritize your tasks, and do not be afraid to decline requests that do not align with your objectives. It's perfectly ok to say no.

THE SUCCESS CHALLENGE #14

1. *Develop a go-to response for declining requests politely. For example, "Thank you for thinking of me, but I'm currently unable to take on any new commitments. Let's revisit this in the future." Practice this response until it feels natural. This will reduce the stress and hesitation and allow you to be respectful when declining requests.*

2. *Reflect on what truly matters to you in both your personal and professional life. Revisit your main goals and the steps needed to achieve them. Use this list as a reference when deciding whether to accept or decline requests.*

3. *When you do receive a new request, take a moment to consider your existing obligations. Ask yourself if you have the time and energy to take on the new task without compromising your current responsibilities. If it doesn't fit, use your polite declination response.*

"Some people are so busy in learning the tricks of the trade that they never learn the trade."

—VERN LAW

Chapter Fifteen

THE TRADE PATH

>—————————<

IT IS NECESSARY to preface this chapter with a disclaimer: College is a wonderful experience, and those with college degrees are truly commendable. Achieving a college degree is a remarkable accomplishment, and I have immense respect for students who dedicate themselves to their academic pursuits.

But...there's another path to success that I discovered, one that does not necessarily require a degree and, therefore, the burden of crushing student loan debt.

This concept took me a while to learn, and once the stigma of "if you don't go to college after high school, then you're basically a failure" mindset was tossed out, I discovered something that has led me to the stairs of success. This discovery is that learning a trade or skill can be more valuable than some college degrees.

The conventional narrative touts the benefits of a college education. However, an alternative route of learning a trade and establishing your own business presents a compelling argument for gaining rapid financial success. There are several reasons why this path might be more advantageous to some than pursuing a traditional college degree.

To state the obvious, one of the primary drawbacks of pursuing a college degree is the significant financial burden it imposes. Tuition fees, textbooks, accommodations, and various other expenses can accumulate into a substantial debt that lingers long after graduation. This financial strain creates the obligation to spend years repaying student loans with ridiculous interest, stifling our ability to put it toward building wealth or investing in our dreams.

On the contrary, learning a trade typically requires a more cost-effective approach. Trade schools or apprenticeships are affordable alternatives to traditional education, allowing us to acquire useful skills without accumulating massive debts. This accessibility provides a more inclusive environment for those seeking skill development without the financial hurdles associated with a college education.

The significant advantage of learning a trade and starting your own business is the *critical demand* for skilled services.

As technology advances, new types of jobs are created, but this shift has also led to a shortage in the skilled trade sector. Many experienced tradesmen are retiring, and there are few skilled tradesmen to replace them, resulting in a severe need for the services. From plumbers to HVAC technicians, mechanics to electricians, skilled trades are more essential than ever, and starting a business in this field offers substantial opportunities for growth and success.

Skilled trades are unfairly viewed as less desirable compared to white-collar careers, which is entirely false on an objective level. Many skilled trades are not only essential but also deeply fulfilling. Each profession plays a vital role in our community, and recognizing the value of all work is crucial for a balanced, respectful society. A garbage service or Honeybucket delivery service is just as essential as an engineer or IT support.

If managed correctly, the viability of skilled trades is a pathway to a very prosperous career. Tradespeople start earning a good income shortly after their training, surpassing the earnings of those with four-year degrees.

One evening, my husband and I went to a hibachi restaurant and sat next to a local couple. As we chatted, they shared their struggles in finding a drywall installation service to complete the homes they were building in a nearby development. They explained that there was only one drywall installation company in the area, and it was booked solid for at least a year.

It was a staggering revelation to learn that the demand for a drywall installer was so high that it brought the progress of a new home development to a standstill because there were no other companies available. The contractors likely considered hiring someone from out of state, but the costs of temporarily housing a crew and covering their travel expenses would have exceeded their budget.

Had I not been wrapped up in my current endeavors, I would have learned everything there is to know about drywall—the material, the cost, how to cut and hang it—and then formed a drywall installation LLC.

No college degree required.

No student loan debt.

Immediate access to the workforce.

Basic startup expenses, licenses, and insurance are

significantly less expensive than college tuition. In my home state of Washington, a *very* rough and basic estimate of starting a drywall installation business would cost approximately $20,000, plus the cost of a work vehicle if needed. According to a quick Google search, the average earnings for drywall installation in a 2,000 sq ft home range from $8,000 to $30,000, depending on the specifics of the job and market conditions.

Clearly, after completing just a few jobs, you would cover your startup expenses and begin generating profit. Again, this is a very vague estimate to convey my point, but you get the idea. The return on investment is evident, making this an incredibly viable and lucrative business opportunity.

No degree and no debt!

Do I love drywall? No. Not at all. But in the name of success, it doesn't matter. What matters most is financial and time freedom. Hypothetically, a few years after this drywall business was established and scaled, I could hire a supervisor to take my place, step out, and let that business purr while I go on to start another venture.

There are careers that require a formal education, and there are careers centered around humanitarian services, *all of which* are important. Each path contributes uniquely to society, whether through specialized knowledge, skilled trades, or compassionate service. I wish I had known this trade path option when I graduated high school, and it's disheartening to know that many schools don't teach this alternative. As the famous quote by John D. Rockefeller goes, "I don't want a nation of thinkers, I want a nation of workers." If that doesn't ruffle your feathers and make you question everything you know about the current system, then I don't know what will. The real problem is that we're educated to repeat what we're taught and not to question what we're taught. It's a slippery slope with many different perspectives and opinions, and all I offer is that you consider hearing alternative voices on the matters before concluding your position.

This issue of the current system strategy to push college after graduation leads to the overlooked trade path as a career option. By promoting trade education alongside traditional academic routes, we could equip young adults with the knowledge and skills to make informed decisions about their futures. It would open doors for many students, providing them with the opportunity to achieve financial stability and give them the chance to buy a house and start a family or have the means to live life the way they want.

It's a complex topic that could take us down a rabbit hole, but I encourage you to research your options before committing to a social narrative and feeling pressured to go to college instead of learning a trade. If you decide that college is the right path for you, know that your choice is equally valid and commendable. Both higher education and trades require dedication and skill, and each can lead to a fulfilling and successful career. All career paths are respected, and we have more opportunities at our fingertips than we will ever know.

THE SUCCESS CHALLENGE #15

1. Even if you're established in your career, take a moment to explore the trade opportunities in your area. Research the average earnings, job prospects, start-up costs, and demand. Now, outline a 5-year projection based on your findings and compare that to your current career earning trajectory. Consider which is a better fit for your financial and success goals.

*2. **If your current career earning trajectory exceeds the potential trade hypothesis, please skip this next step.** If there is an earning potential that exceeds your career earnings, seek out opportunities to gain hands-on experience in a chosen trade through internships, apprenticeships, or volunteer work. Network with professionals and gain insights into the trade industry.*

3. Invest in trade education and training and take the next steps toward enrolling in a program that prepares you for a chosen field. Follow The Success Challenge actionable steps that you've learned so far and apply them toward your newly established trade business goal.

"Don't take advice from anyone you wouldn't trade places with."

—NAVAL RAVIKANT

Chapter Sixteen

BE WARY OF DANGEROUS ADVICE

>———————————<

ADVICE IS EVERYWHERE. Someone has a shortcut for you that can make your life easier. Someone else has a workshop to teach you the secret to whatever it is you're doing. There are podcasts, YouTube channels, social media channels, and just about any platform to spread the word of unsolicited advice on a topic that you never thought you'd need. There are so many voices who want to share their experience based on their personal worldview. That is when things can become dangerous if we listen to the wrong voices.

How do you distinguish between helpful and harmful guidance? What can we do to navigate the digital noise and make informed choices about which advice we take?

Using common sense and logic to filter through what is being shared is the starting point at which we can begin. Ask yourself if what they're saying is too good to be true, and always, *always* question their sources. Where did the information come from? Is the information factual or based upon their truths? There is no such thing as a stupid question, so by doing your due diligence and researching, allow yourself the freedom to ask the questions that will give you a better understanding of the information you're absorbing and make informed choices through this.

It's important to note that I wouldn't be where I am today without the help and guidance of worksheets, workshops, channels, and social media accounts. They have helped me to navigate the challenges of marketing and pulling everything together. I relied heavily on many voices in the industry, and I've come to find out that some of the voices I admired were no less than a fake guru, pretending to share that their methods were foolproof. It's heartbreaking, really, to think that I spent hours watching YouTube tutorials from people who had written a terrible book and contradicted themselves by posting content that was completely backwards from what they drilled-in the week before.

Within my "authorpreneurship" journey, there has been one particularly bad apple in the bunch, and it cost me a lot of time, frustration, and thousands of wasted dollars. It all started on LinkedIn when I received a message from a young lady who claimed to be a highly successful entrepreneur. She told me that she could help female entrepreneurs just like me create massive visibility by creating and developing my personal brand and marketing strategy to scale my business fast.

She sounded friendly enough, so I took the bait. I messaged back and thanked her for reaching out, and I began to tell her about my experience as an author. Unsure if her coaching would apply to me and my author brand, I asked if she'd worked with other authors before.

Her response was quick, and she told me we had so much in common. She was featured in a collaborated book with other female entrepreneurs, and she claimed to be writing a book on personal branding.

Sounds great, right? I continued to read on.

This woman dropped her hook about her online training program, which would take me through the process of creating my author brand, logo, marketing messages, strategy, website, funnels, and more.

It was everything I was looking for and needed at the time. I was in the process of writing my own online workshop for aspiring writers, and she had my full attention. I booked a 1:1 phone call to discuss the details of her program and how she can help me. I was thrilled!

The next week, I answered her phone call. She had a lovely, thick British accent and said all the right things. I explained to her my goals, struggles, and where I wanted to be in the next five years. She insisted she was the right person to help me, and I was genuinely sold. Well, almost. I wanted to discuss it with my husband first because of the large financial investment, and I wanted to gather his thoughts to ensure I wasn't buying something impulsively.

Then, I was ready to take the plunge.

I paid the woman $2,000 and printed everything from the receipts, email conversations, and her contact information. She sounded so damn LEGIT. Her LinkedIn profile showed a picture of her standing next to a giant clock tower, and she was wearing a hot pink business suit with the text "FOX news interview" and the date of the upcoming feature. I remember thinking, WOW, she will be interviewed by FOX, and she'll be on TV! That's someone who I want to learn from, and I want to build my platform like her.

Now, here's where I made my fatal flaw.

I compared myself to someone based on a social

media photo. I judged her success by a stupid picture on her profile. That's how gullible I was and how much my emotions led me on. This is a lesson that I wish to go back in time and tell myself to watch out for: refrain from looking at social media as a measure of success.

It is absolutely, positively false.

Nearly everything on social media is fake. Think about it; even some of my own photos have a filter that makes my skin appear smoother or my lashes longer! Social media has become an outlet to share our accomplishments and the great things that happened to us in exchange for digital accolades. Only the things that would generate a reaction from the public (or friends and family) are posted because they garner likes and comments, making us feel good. That's a dangerous road to walk down because we cannot differentiate between real and exaggerated.

This woman set me up with a login through the Teachable platform, and I was thrilled to get started. The course was set up in a "drip" format, where I would get the first module, take a week to complete it, and, upon completion, the next module would be unlocked. This way, I wouldn't be able to burn through the entire course, and I would pace myself to learn and do the exercises fully.

I was so excited that I went to the store and bought a cute binder and some supplies to organize my course content. If there ever was a time that I embraced the idea of learning and dedicated myself to the outcome, this was it.

The first task was to watch a welcome video. Now, I'm not a professional and I don't believe you need professional equipment to create a video, but her recordings looked to be the same quality as a Zoom call. Remember, I spent TWO THOUSAND DOLLARS on this course, and I got to watch a crappy video about everything I had already studied in great depth. She was talking about having a positive mindset, and healthy habits. She talked about creating a vision board (and tagging her on Instagram when I posted it. HA!) and all about the healthy habits of successful people. At that point, it felt like I was a college grad sitting in a Kindergarten classroom. Why would she start her advanced coaching course like that? If you're searching for success, it's a commandment that we exercise positive thinking and disciplined thinking and understand that we can manifest anything we desire.

She repeated all the entry-level information.

Money is infinite, and whatever we focus on, we attract. The law of attraction. I already read several (and I mean SEVERAL) books about this topic. I watched every Tony Robbins video, Les Brown, and the Motivation Madness channel on YouTube. I was very well acquainted with this concept.

Okay, maybe someone who was enrolled in her course wasn't familiar with it. But based on what she had been selling me in the beginning during our phone conversation, I was beyond the point she had been referring to in her welcome video. I was basically getting a refresher course in mindset. Nothing wrong with that, I suppose. Maybe I was just too eager to get some answers to my questions, so I was patient and took it seriously.

I jumped in with both feet. I did the first exercise, printed a blank check, wrote it to myself for a million dollars, and signed it from the Universe. I cut up magazines to create my vision board and dreamed of the house I would purchase if, no *when* I had the money. I posted it on social media, tagged her, and kept every scrap of paper in my binder. I completely and utterly immersed myself in this course, because she promised to give me the directions to creating a brand and launching my online course that would rake in millions.

It makes me angry to think how she duped me.

I got through the first week. Then, the second week. At this point, I'd learned nothing new that I hadn't already learned from YouTube and countless books.

Then came the third week.

I logged in to the dashboard and checked for the next module. Interestingly, the "drip" video hadn't dripped. I sent a quick message to her inbox with a heads-up that the module hadn't been posted, and I waited.

And waited.

Ten days later, I still hadn't heard back, and I was beginning to worry. There were fresh posts on her socials, so I knew she was active but maybe she missed my email. So, I tried again.

And waited.

Another two weeks passed, and I hadn't heard anything from this woman, and my heart sank. Deep down, I knew she was fake. All those posts on her social media? Fake. Her supposed success? Fake. It became apparent that the images she was posting gave the impression that she was a highfalutin traveler of the world when, in fact, she was just an average person working for a particular MLM company, pretending to be someone she was not.

Trying to get my money back was a total loss at that point. My messages were read but not answered. I remember getting so angry at the level of disappointment I felt because I had believed in someone. Not only was that person misleading me, but how many others had also been snared in her trap of lies?

It was a hard lesson to learn, but my approach to evaluating professionals has drastically changed. Now, I thoroughly research anyone claiming to be an expert before considering their advice. This diligent scrutiny has enabled me to filter out harmful voices and highlight the helpful ones. Always ask questions, check sources, and listen with a curious and discerning heart.

When receiving advice from someone you know, remember that you have the power to assess how they manage their own lifestyle and the choices they make. Often, people give advice based on their personal experiences and belief systems, which may not align with yours. For instance, you wouldn't take relationship advice from someone who has been divorced five times. Similarly, it's unwise to accept financial advice from someone who is sinking into debt due to poor financial decisions. Instead, seek out voices with proven results that back up their claims. We're all striving for success, so find the individuals who have achieved what you aspire to. They are the ones with valuable and actionable advice. In this way, you practice common sense, logic, and reasoning, discerning what is truly beneficial. Don't fall into the trap of believing everything you see on social media. It's not all that it appears to be.

THE SUCCESS CHALLENGE #16

1. Take a critical look at where you are gathering your information. Investigate the backgrounds of the influencers you follow and determine if their success is due to genuine hard work or merely social media popularity. Do they have a documented history that shows their evolution into success? Look for tangible evidence of their achievements and the journey they took to get there. This will help you distinguish between superficial success and authentic, hard-earned expertise.

2. Reflect on the advice you receive from friends, family, and acquaintances. Consider their track record and lifestyle choices. Are they offering guidance based on personal success or their own unresolved struggles? Prioritize advice from those who embody the outcomes you desire. Create a checklist to evaluate the credibility of advice: does the advisor have practical experience, consistent results, and values that align with your goals? By doing this, you ensure that the guidance you follow is not only well-intentioned but also effective and relevant to your own path to success.

"You can only expand your capacities by working to the very limit."

—HUGH NIBLEY

Chapter Seventeen

EXPAND YOUR CAPACITY

>———————<

SELF-IMPOSED LIMITS are the invisible barriers we construct around ourselves when we believe we cannot achieve something. They form a ceiling that we stand beneath, feeling content and comfortable in our constrained space. When opportunities call, we can't hear them because we are trapped within this box of limitations.

The primary reason we place these limits on ourselves is fear. Fear of failure, fear of the unknown, and fear of stepping outside our comfort zones. It can be so paralyzing that it convinces us to stay within the familiar, even if it means stunting our growth. Additionally, societal expectations and past experiences can reinforce these self-imposed limits, making us believe that we are not capable of achieving more than what we currently have.

However, these barriers are often based on perceptions rather than reality. By challenging them, we can begin to expand our capacity and unlock new potential. The first step is to recognize these limits for what they are—constructs of our own minds. Once identified, we can start dismantling them by setting small, achievable goals that push us slightly beyond our comfort zones.

I have to admit, I absolutely hate working out. Running, in particular, feels like pure torture. If something were chasing me, I'd probably prefer to be caught rather than run. However, recognizing the importance of physical fitness for maintaining a healthy body, I decided to make a change. I bought a treadmill and started my fitness journey.

It started out slow, just walking for twenty minutes while listening to music. I'd bump up the speed to a running pace and commit myself to misery for about 45 seconds before punching the decrease-speed button and gasping for air as if I'd drowned. For a while, that's how I would maintain my workout. Just to the point of discomfort, and then I'd stop.

I had been listening to an audiobook by David Goggins, a former Navy SEAL and ultramarathon runner who transformed his life through sheer mental toughness. His story of overcoming immense physical and mental challenges resonated deeply with me and inspired me to make a change in my own life. I mean, there's just something about an angry, passionate man yelling at you to suck it up and be tough. It's not for everyone, but at the time, it was exactly what I needed.

My next workout session started out by walking to warm up, and I mentally prepared myself for what I was about to do. I thought to myself repeatedly, "*This is what we're doing. We're going to do this. WE ARE DOING THIS.*" The mantra became my focus, setting my intention firmly.

Then, I bumped the speed up to a jog.

I made it through 45 seconds.

Then, another 45 seconds.

My body screamed at me to slow down, but I just repeated my mantra, "*This is what we're doing. We're going to do this. WE ARE DOING THIS.*"

Incredibly, I blanked my mind and found that my jogging pace matched the beat of the music I was listening to. I took deep breaths to recalibrate and found a rhythm to my breathing. When the song was over, I glanced down at the dashboard and saw that I had been jogging for *four minutes*.

Triumphant, I slowed it down to a brisk walk, feeling the burn in my lungs and the ache in my legs. But it felt so good. I had done it!

I had expanded my capacity.

That limiting belief that I could only run for less than a minute was shattered when I overrode my mental system.

I told my body what to do, and it listened.

The sense of accomplishment was so great that I craved it again. I took another minute to catch my breath and did it all over again.

This time, I jogged for *five* minutes.

Today, I've expanded my capacity to 45 minutes on the treadmill, followed by a Pilates routine. Each day, I push my limit by adding an extra minute, an extra rep, or burning more calories than the day before. This progressive challenge has improved not only my physical fitness but also my mental resilience. I've developed a greater sense of self-discipline and confidence by continuously striving to expand my capacity.

This experience taught me that the barriers we set for ourselves are often just mental constructs. When we push past these perceived limits, we can witness the infinite abilities within us. Each small victory builds upon the last, creating a powerful momentum that leads to the results we want. This concept applies to every aspect of life.

In his book, *Can't Hurt Me: Master Your Mind and Defy the Odds*, Goggins introduces the concept of the "40% Rule." This rule suggests that when you think you are completely exhausted and have reached your limit, you are actually only at 40% of your true potential. Think of it as pouring a glass of water and believing it to be full at just 40%. Tip it back and pour again!

In daily life, this principle applies to more than just physical challenges. Whether it's taking on a demanding project at work, learning a new skill, or overcoming a personal fear, the process of expanding our capacity involves pushing beyond our comfort zones. You've got to embrace discomfort and know that it's *only* when we reach our limits and take a step beyond that growth happens.

When you come home from school or work feeling tired, and you flop onto the couch, mindlessly scrolling through social media, you're not doing yourself any favors. You might think you're too exhausted to do anything productive, but in reality, you're perfectly capable of working on that project you started.

Whenever I hear people say they can't do something because it looks too hard or they're too tired, my heart sinks because they're making a subconscious choice to limit themselves. Statements like, "I'm not good at math" or "I could never start a business" are expressions of self-imposed limits that people place on themselves. When people declare their inability to do something without even attempting it, they confine themselves within the boundaries of what they perceive as possible.

These mental barriers prevent growth and achievement. They create a false narrative of incapability. To overcome these barriers, challenge your limiting beliefs and push beyond your comfort zone. Recognize the excuses you make for yourself and replace them with action.

Expand your capacity!

One effective way to start expanding your capacity is to set incremental goals. Just as I added a minute to my treadmill time, you can break down your larger objectives into manageable steps. Celebrate each achievement and use it as motivation to keep going.

When you make the conscious decision to

conquer self-imposed limits and expand your capacity, you unleash your true potential and transform not just your abilities but your entire life. Embrace the challenge, push past the fear, and watch as you achieve more than you ever imagined possible.

THE SUCCESS CHALLENGE #17

1. Very simply, in your daily tasks, expand your capacity and conquer self-imposed limits. Push yourself beyond what you think is possible. In small increments, add more when you feel as though you've hit a wall. For instance, if you're used to reading for 30 minutes, extend it to 35 minutes. If you typically lift 10 pounds during workouts, try lifting 11. Replace negative thoughts with affirmations like, "I am capable of learning and improving." Create your own mantra and speak it loudly within your mind.

2. Identify one small challenge daily that makes you uncomfortable. This could be as simple as starting a conversation with a stranger, trying a new hobby, or taking on a new responsibility at work. Regularly pushing your boundaries helps desensitize you to discomfort, making it easier to tackle larger challenges in the future.

"Some people grumble that
roses have thorns;
I am grateful that thorns
have roses."

—ALPHONSE KARR

Chapter Eighteen

GRATITUDE ATTITUDE

>———————————<

GRATITUDE IS THE lens through which life becomes richer and more fulfilling. It can be an attitude or a point of view, but either way is transformative.

I grew up as a "valley girl" in a comfortable part of Spokane, Washington. Everything I needed was within a 10-minute drive from grocery stores to parks, schools to shopping; convenience was a hallmark of my childhood. Life in Spokane was easy and predictable. I lived in a bubble of comfort and familiarity, and luxuries were abundant.

In this environment, it was easy to take things for granted. The convenience of my surroundings meant I rarely had to step out of my comfort zone. My world was small and safe, but I felt that it lacked depth. At the time, I didn't realize how much I was missing out on by not fully appreciating the blessings around me. Still, I wanted more, not appreciating that I already had so much to be grateful for.

It wasn't until I moved three hours away from my comfortable city life to my husband's little hometown to build our home on a raw piece of land that I truly understood the power of gratitude.

The transition was nothing short of drastic. Total culture shock and the sinking feeling of homesickness plagued me.

Gone were the days of quick errands and spontaneous meetups with friends. Instead, I faced a new reality: a solitary house standing on acres of undeveloped land, surrounded by nothing but grassy hills, mountains, and open sky. Everything was new and unfamiliar, and initially, it all seemed terrible.

The first few months were the hardest. The silence was deafening, and I missed the sound of birds chirping. There were no close neighbors to chat with, no friends to visit, and family was hours away. The nearest store was about 25 miles in each direction, turning simple shopping trips into excursions. I found myself missing the convenience and the social connections of my old life. The isolation felt overwhelming, and I wondered if I had made a mistake.

Yet, during this upheaval, something incredible began to happen. The vast open spaces that once seemed intimidating started to feel liberating. The silence that initially felt oppressive became therapeutic. The discovery of new sounds—the rustle of leaves, the songs of different birds, the whisper of the wind. These subtle noises began to soothe my city-worn soul.

I began to appreciate the process of setting up our home from scratch. It was a symbol of our new beginning and the embodiment of our dreams. Each day, I woke up to a golden sunrise, and at night, I looked up at a swath of stars—the Milky Way itself! —and I began to feel a growing sense of pride and gratitude.

Slowly, my perspective started to shift. Instead of focusing on what I had left behind, I began to see the beauty and potential in my new surroundings. The countryside offered tranquility and a connection to nature that I had never experienced before. I found joy in simple pleasures. Morning walks through dew-kissed fields, evenings spent stargazing, chasing the pesky deer away from my doorstep...

Gratitude became my guide.

When I stopped thinking about what I lost, I started thinking about what I was so fortunate to have. It taught me to value the present moment and enjoy the simplicity of everyday life. I started keeping a gratitude journal, jotting down three things I was thankful for each day. This simple practice shifted my focus from what I lacked to what I had, which gave me a sense of relief from all of the negative thoughts.

My mind grew quiet.

My body relaxed.

I felt *content*.

This shift happened when I internalized my gratitude for these things. There's a certain feeling associated with being grateful. I would reflect on something simple, such as the moon, allowing myself to fully immerse in contemplation of its presence. I would think about how many people throughout history have gazed upon this very moon, and that feeling of amazement and appreciation would start to grow. I'd hold onto that feeling and let it deepen, considering the moon's constant presence and the shared human experience it represents.

Gratitude is not just about saying thank you but about seeing the value of the gifts or blessings in our lives. After recognizing the abundance that exists in every moment and appreciating the simple joys that we overlook, gratitude will transform your life.

A happy life is not in what we possess but in how we perceive and appreciate what we have. You can't be negative when you're grateful. It's simply not possible.

The drastic change from city life to country living initially felt like a loss, but it became a profound gain. Building our home wasn't just about creating a physical space; it was about creating a new mindset. The solitude and challenges taught me resilience, the natural beauty taught me appreciation, and the slower pace taught me patience. Ultimately, gratitude became the foundation upon which my new life was built.

Feel grateful for what you have, even the simplest things, such as a comfortable chair to sit in, a cup to drink from, or a warm bed to sleep in. Appreciate the roof over your head that provides shelter, the food on your table that nourishes you, and the clean water you can access every day. Instead of complaining about our jobs, we should switch to gratitude and be thankful for the opportunity to be employed, which allows us to provide for ourselves and our families.

Recognize the beauty in the small joys of life—a kind smile from a stranger, a good book to read, or the sun's warmth on your face. With gratitude, you will rewire your brain to focus on the positives in your life and increase your sense of well-being and happiness.

THE SUCCESS CHALLENGE #18

1. Practice gratitude by setting aside a few minutes daily to write down three things you are grateful for. Choose a specific time of day, such as in the morning or before bed, and commit to writing in your journal regularly. These can be simple things, like a beautiful sunset, a kind gesture, or a delicious meal. The key is consistency. Reflect deeply on these three things and internalize them. Allow yourself to truly feel gratitude and absorb the appreciation fully.

2. Choose something you're grateful for, such as hot water, the internet, or a dishwasher. Then, go 24 hours without that item. As you go about your day, reflect on the impact its absence has on your routine. Notice the inconveniences that arise without it and consider how profoundly it contributes to your daily life. This will deepen your appreciation for the conveniences you often take for granted, highlighting their significance and enhancing your sense of gratitude.

"Your mental health is a priority. Your self-care is a priority. Your happiness is a priority. Your existence is a priority."

—OLIVIA JADE

Chapter Nineteen

SELF-CARE

>————————<

SELF-CARE IS MORE than just bubble baths and spa days. It's a holistic approach to nurturing your physical, mental, emotional, and spiritual well-being.

Many of us have been conditioned to believe that self-sacrifice is noble or virtuous, but I challenge that idea. Self-care is a necessary foundation for prioritizing your own needs without guilt or shame. By taking care of yourself, you ensure that you have the energy, strength, and health needed to support your ambitions. If you're not your best self, then you cannot effectively operate at peak performance.

Think of self-care as tending to a garden. Each aspect of your well-being represents a different type of plant, and for your garden to flourish, you have to care for all of them.

Your physical health is like the soil, providing the

essential nutrients your body needs through regular exercise, a healthy, balanced diet, and a good night's sleep.

Poor soil leads to weak plants, just as neglecting your physical health can lead to poor overall well-being. When the garden soil lacks nutrients, we mix in fresh, healthy, organic soil to replace the depleted dirt. Similarly, when your body is neglected, it requires replenishment through healthier habits. Incorporating nutrient-rich foods, maintaining a consistent exercise routine, and ensuring a good night's sleep can rejuvenate your body, just like enriching the soil refreshes a garden. Proper hydration, regular medical check-ups, and mindful practices contribute to maintaining this "soil" so that your physical foundation is strong and capable of supporting your overall health.

Mental health is like the sunlight, vital for helping plants thrive. Finding activities that stimulate your mind keeps your mental faculties sharp. Cognitive growth enhances problem-solving abilities and boosts creativity, which leads to innovation. Just as plants lean towards sunlight for optimal growth, your mind seeks out stimulation to remain healthy. Regular mental exercise, like daily sunlight exposure for plants, ensures that your cognitive functions remain strong, helping you adapt to new situations, think critically, and maintain emotional balance.

It's important to acknowledge that seeking help for mental health is a sign of strength, not weakness. Asking for support requires courage, and there's no shame in reaching out to professionals or loved ones when needed. Prioritizing mental health is paramount, and it is the most important aspect to focus on above everything else discussed in this book.

Emotional health is watering your garden. Just as water is crucial for plants to grow, acknowledging and processing your emotions is essential for maintaining emotional health. Water nourishes plants, helping them absorb nutrients from the soil and sustain life. Similarly, emotional health involves recognizing, understanding, and expressing your feelings, which nurtures your overall well-being. Suppressing emotions can lead to a build-up of stress and anxiety, much like how a lack of water can cause plants to wilt and die. Regularly addressing your emotions prevents negative feelings from accumulating and ensures a healthier state of mind. Talking to a friend, journaling your thoughts, or meditation are wonderful outlets for sorting through our feelings. Consistent emotional care allows you to process experiences, manage stress, and enjoy life.

Finally, spiritual health is the air your garden breathes. This can be nurtured through various practices depending on your personal beliefs, each offering unique benefits. Attending church services and worship provides a deep sense of connection and peace. Other practices of spiritual health, like using crystals, harness natural energies for healing and connection. Meditation and mindfulness quiet the mind and promote inner peace, and spending time in nature offers rest and grounding. Creative activities like art, music, and writing can also serve as spiritual outlets, allowing you to express your innermost thoughts and feelings and connect with a deeper part of yourself. Prioritizing spiritual health ensures your inner garden thrives, enriching your overall well-being.

By caring for each facet of yourself, you create a balanced and thriving garden. A healthy body, mind, heart, and soul is what will allow you to achieve peak performance and lead a fulfilling life.

There's no shame in self-preservation. Take care of yourself!

THE SUCCESS CHALLENGE #19

1. *Stick to a consistent exercise schedule that fits your lifestyle. Create a weekly menu that supports a healthy diet and use moderation for the unnecessary treats that don't serve your physical health.*

2. *Dedicate time to reading, working on a puzzle, or learning a new skill at least once a day. Keep your mind active and replace social media scrolling with one of these activities.*

3. *Practice emotional health by journaling and participating in activities that bring you joy and relaxation. If needed, seek support from a therapist or counselor to navigate emotional challenges.*

4. *Actively participate in your spiritual practices as often as necessary to maintain inner peace. Depending on your beliefs, apply it to a consistent schedule and commit to those practices.*

"Do not wait; the time will never be just right. Start where you stand, and work with whatever tools you may have at your command, and better tools will be found as you go along."

—NAPOLEON HILL

Chapter Twenty

THE SUCCESS CHALLENGE

>———————————<

SUCCESS IS NOT a one-time achievement but a continuous journey of growth, learning, and improvement. Its definition is limitless and subjective, varying depending on who defines it. For some, success is reaching career milestones, while for others, it's personal fulfillment or making a positive impact on the community. This ongoing pursuit encourages us to set new goals, embrace challenges, and strive for excellence in all areas of life while understanding that each step forward, no matter how small, contributes to our overall success.

It all starts when you redefine success.

That's when the shift happens. Your mindset becomes focused, positive, and prepared for overcoming setbacks. With a new perspective on success, you're better equipped to handle the inevitable challenges that arise on your path. You start seeing failures as learning opportunities, and each hurdle is just another rung on the ladder toward your ultimate goals.

You surround yourself with people who encourage your growth and support your dreams, and you drift away from those who drag you down. Soon, you find a mentor who embodies the success you aspire to and follow their guidance, learning from their wisdom and mistakes. As you absorb their lessons and apply them to your goals, you start to see tangible progress, further fueling your determination and commitment to your redefined vision of success.

You outline your goals and break them down into smaller, manageable steps. With your assigned deadlines, you begin to work out a schedule to accomplish each task with consistency and momentum.

Meanwhile, you're reviewing your financial situation and creating a budget, accounting for each penny earned and spent. You're on track to have your debt paid off, and you've saved an emergency fund for any potential obstacles. This financial discipline provides a sense of security and frees up mental space, allowing you to focus more intently on your goals.

You show up all day, every day, and develop a habit of consistency. The payoff for this is exponential, and you are closer to your goals than ever before. Even though times are tough, you stick to it and maintain self-discipline, preparing for that sweet, delayed gratification.

Your network has grown, and your access to information has helped you to step even closer to your goals. You're equipped with the resources, and there are several opportunities you're exploring that arose from your new connections.

Even though you're stepping into uncharted waters, you do so with confidence. Leveraging your strengths and staying authentic to your true self, you believe in yourself and in your abilities. Several doors open, and you decide which one will bring you closer to your goal.

You treat yourself to little rewards as you reach each milestone, and you're excited for the big reward when you accomplish your goal. That little flame of motivation burns with each small achievement, and you push forward.

Some setbacks have occurred, but you embrace them as learning opportunities. You're afraid, but you have identified that your fear is simply a response to a narrative in your mind, and you correct it by changing the way you think about it.

Your distractions are at a minimum because you've politely turned down several commitments that would have crossed your protected time and energy boundaries. With a clear schedule and a focused mindset, you push forward toward your goal.

Your mind is exploring trade opportunities and lucrative investments, researching ways that can elevate your financial sustainability. You discover that your area has a need for a trade that you're particularly interested in, and you begin outlining a business plan.

Even though you're tired and would rather indulge in mindless activities, you press on because you've conquered self-imposed limits and expanded your capacity. You can do anything, and you are confident in yourself.

Things look great because you feel grateful for what you have accomplished so far. Your positive outlook has kept your focus clear, preventing the negative space from clouding your mind and judgment.

Knowing you cannot pour from an empty cup, you prioritize self-care and practice healthy routines that nurture your physical, mental, emotional, and spiritual well-being. You look amazing, feel amazing, and you can take on the stress of the final steps of your goal.

With each passing day, you work toward your redefined version of success. You're achieving your goals and becoming the best version of yourself, and you're inspiring those around you to strive for their own greatness. You've built a life that reflects your values, ambitions, and dreams, and this is just the beginning. There will always be new goals to set, new horizons to explore, and new heights to reach for.

You've learned the secret to winning *The Success Challenge* because you chose to take that first step and kept going to the end. Your determination, perseverance, and commitment to growth have led you to this moment of triumph. You've proven that success is a passage of relentless effort and self-belief by continually pushing yourself, embracing challenges, and maintaining a positive outlook.

Now close your eyes and manifest this outcome, keeping it close to your heart and sparking the fire of motivation.

Once you feel it, sit with it, and soak it up.

Let this vision of success fuel your determination and guide your actions. Embrace the journey ahead with confidence, knowing that you have the strength to achieve anything you focus your mind on. Your future is bright, and your journey is far from over. The possibilities ahead are limitless. Soon, you can look back and tell someone that it all started when you *redefined* success.

And your results will speak loudly enough.

The Success Challenge
RECOMMENDED READING

>————————————<

- ❑ "*Developing the Leader Within You*" by John C. Maxwell: Focuses on developing leadership skills and becoming an effective leader in various aspects of life.

- ❑ *Psycho-Cybernetics*, by Maxwell Maltz: Explores the concept of self-image and its impact on success and happiness.

- ❑ *Awaken the Giant Within*, by Tony Robbins: Empowers readers to take control of their lives, emotions, finances, and relationships through practical strategies.

- ❑ *Can't Hurt Me*, by David Goggins: A memoir of overcoming obstacles, developing mental toughness, and achieving greatness.

- ❏   *The Total Money Makeover*, by Dave Ramsey: A step-by-step guide to financial fitness, offering a practical plan for getting out of debt and building wealth.

- ❏   *EntreLeadership*, by Dave Ramsey: Combines the principles of entrepreneurship and leadership to provide a guide for building a successful business.

- ❏   *Think and Grow Rich*, by Napoleon Hill: A classic book on personal development and success principles, outlining the philosophy of success and the principles to achieve it.

- ❏   *How to Win Friends and Influence People*, by Dale Carnegie: A guide to improving interpersonal skills and building relationships, providing timeless principles for effective communication.

- ❏   *Rich Dad Poor Dad*, by Robert T. Kiyosaki: A personal finance classic that contrasts the financial philosophies of the author's two "dads" and provides insights on wealth-building.

- *The Magic of Thinking Big*, by David J. Schwartz: Encourages readers to set high goals and believe in their ability to achieve them, offering practical advice for success and personal growth.

- *Choose Your Enemies Wisely*, by Patrick Bet-David: Focuses on understanding the dynamics of competition and conflict, and how choosing the right opponents can lead to personal growth.

- *The 10X Rule*, by Grant Cardone: Encourages readers to set goals 10 times higher than they think they can achieve and to take massive action to achieve them.

- *The Success Principles*, by Jack Canfield: A comprehensive guide to achieving success, with 64 principles that can help you achieve your goals.

- *Good to Great*, by Jim Collins: Examines how good companies can become great companies, identifying key factors that contribute to sustained success.

- *The Slight Edge*, by Jeff Olson: Explains how making simple daily disciplines can lead to success and happiness.

- *Start with Why*, by Simon Sinek: Explains how great leaders inspire action by focusing on the "why" behind their actions.

- *The Compound Effect*, by Darren Hardy: Explains how small, consistent actions can lead to significant results over time, emphasizing the power of compounding in growth.

- *The Go-Giver*, by Bob Burg and John David Mann: A parable that teaches the power of giving and how it can lead to success in business and life.

- *Who Moved My Cheese?*, by Spencer Johnson: A parable that reveals profound truths about dealing with change in work and life.

- *The Lean Startup*, by Eric Ries: Provides a methodology for developing businesses and products through continuous innovation and feedback.

- *Atomic Habits,* by James Clear: Offers a proven framework for building good habits and breaking bad ones.

- *Mindset,* by Carol S. Dweck: Explores the power of a growth mindset and how it can lead to success and fulfillment.

- *Daring Greatly,* by Brené Brown: Examines the power of vulnerability and how it can lead to a more courageous and meaningful life.

- *The 5 Love Languages,* by Gary Chapman: Explains the five love languages and how understanding them can improve relationships.

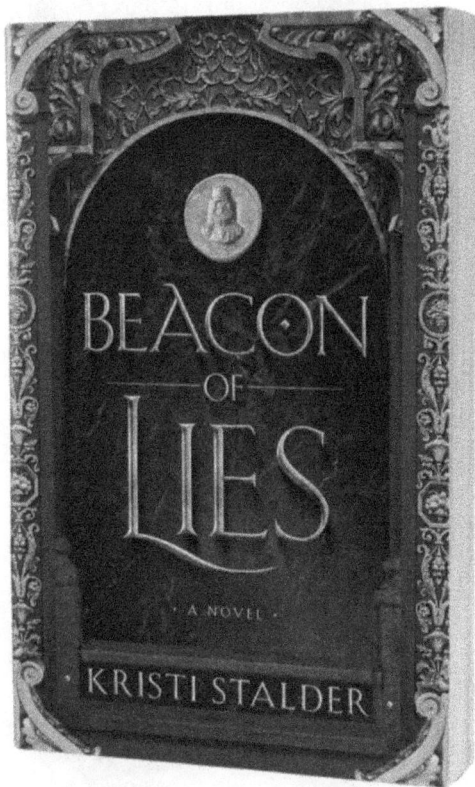

FOR MORE INFORMATION, VISIT:
WWW.KRISTISTALDER.COM

About the Author

Kristi Stalder is an award-winning author and publisher living in a small town in Washington with her kids, horses, and handsome husband. She is certified in Entrepreneurship Essentials from Harvard Business School Online and loves mentoring aspiring writers.

Drawing on her experience as a business owner, Kristi's nonfiction writing reflects a wealth of expertise. Her children's books are inspired by her favorite life lessons through Stoic philosophy, while her fiction showcases her creativity. When not absorbed in the latest gripping page-turner, Kristi enjoys doodling, baking from scratch, and horseback riding all over the countryside.

To explore her world, visit www.KristiStalder.com or find her on social media @AuthorKristiStalder.